ST

verdun

THE AUTHOR

David Mason was born in Brighton in 1969. Having completed his degree, he gained a master's degree from the University of London, and now teaches as a visiting lecturer in history at the University of North London. His interest in World War I was sparked when he learnt that two of his great uncles fought and died in Kitchener's Army. This is David Mason's first book.

Titles in the GREAT BATTLES series

Military History published by The Windrush Press

verdun

DAVID MASON

THE WINDRUSH PRESS · GLOUCESTERSHIRE

First published in Great Britain by
The Windrush Press in 2000
Little Window, High Street,
Moreton-in-Marsh,
Gloucestershire GL56 OLL
Tel: 01608 652012
Fax: 01608 652125 Email: Windrush@windrushpress.com
Website: www.windrushpress.com

British Library in Cataloguing Data
A catalogue record for this book is available from the British Library

ISBN 1 900624 41 9

Cover design Miranda Harvey

Maps by John Taylor

Typeset by Archetype IT Ltd, website: www.archetype-it.com

Printed by Bell & Bain Ltd, Glasgow, UK

To order your free Windrush Press catalogue featuring general
history, military books, travel books, and other titles,
please phone us on
01608 652012 or 01608 652025
Fax us on 01608 652125 Email: Windrush@windrushpress.com
Website: **www.windrushpress.com**
Or write to:
The Windrush Press Limited
Little Window, High Street, Moreton-in-Marsh
Gloucestershire, GL56 OLL, UK

To my father, and Mary Anne, with thanks for their help on both sides of the Channel.

Contents

Author's Acknowledgements

I would like to thank the following people who helped me in the preparation of this book: Victoria Huxley, Professor Denis Judd, Roy Beddes, Peter Smith, Paul and Kathleen Sheehan, Kevin Smith and Rachel Gibson, John Corcoran, and Mary Anne Nelson Cruz. I would also like to thank my parents and family for all their support, and give a special mention to Oliver Stevenson, Billie May, and Joe Baines-Holmes.

List of Illustrations, Maps, and Plans

The ossuary at Douaumont, final resting place for the
unidentified dead of the Verdun battlefield.

MAPS AND BATTLEPLANS

The Battle of Verdun:
A Chronology

1915

6 December   Military conference of Entente Powers at Chantilly. Agreement reached for action against the Central Powers on all fronts in 1916, including Franco-British action in the west.

15 December   Falkenhayn's memorandum to the Kaiser, in which he outlines proposals for attacking the French at Verdun.

1916

January   German preparations for Operation *Gericht* ahead of Verdun. Some 1200 artillery pieces are assembled for the attack.

12 February   Poor weather conditions cause the postponement of *Gericht*.

21 February   German offensive commences on the right bank of the Meuse. A million shells are expended. Infantry advance violates the French line at Bois d'Haumont.

22 February   Fall of Haumont village and Bois des Caures.

23 February   Following the loss of Bois d'Herbebois, Brabant is abandoned, leaving the Germans in almost total possession of the initial French first line. French artillery targets own infantry at Samogneux. German forces later occupy the village, breaking the intermediary line of defence.

24 February   Fall of Beaumont. German gains for the day surpass all others to date.

25 February   Capture of Fort Douaumont. General de Castlenau decides that Verdun can be saved, and orders the continuing defence of positions on both banks of the Meuse.

26 February   French Second Army ordered to Verdun. Pétain takes over command of the region. The 'Line of Resistance' is enacted and communications between the rest of France and the city are reorganized (*Voie Sacrée*).

4 March   Following a week of ferocious fighting, Douaumont village falls.

6 March   German offensive towards Mort Homme on the left bank. Villages of Forges and Regneville fall; Height 265 is occupied.

9 March   Germans claim capture of Fort Vaux.

20 March   Bois d'Avocourt overrun.

10 April   Following containment of concerted attack on Mort Homme, Pétain tells his troops, '*Courage, on les aura!*'

1 May   Pétain takes control of Central Armies Group HQ. Nivelle assumes command at Verdun, promising '*ils ne passeront pas*'.

5 May   The 'Line of Resistance' is broken on the left bank following the loss of Côte 304. By the end of the month, German forces have also occupied Mort Homme and the village of Cumières.

8 May   An explosion within Fort Douaumont leaves some 650 dead.

22 May   Mangin leads a failed attack aimed at reclaiming Fort Douaumont.

1 June   Renewed German offensive on the right bank.

4 June   Russians attack Austro-Hungarian forces on the Eastern Front (the Brusilov Offensive). Falkenhayn is forced to redeploy troops from the west, causing the temporary suspension of the offensive at Verdun.

7 June   Fort Vaux surrendered after a five-day siege. The order is given to instigate the 'Line of Panic'.

11 June   Pétain warns, 'Verdun must not fall'.

22 June   German artillery offensive begins as a prelude to assault on Fort Souville, the last major obstacle between the attacking force and Verdun.

23 June   The village of Fleury becomes the focus of bitter infantry combat.

1 July   British and French forces attack at the Somme.

9 July   Final German effort on Verdun in the direction of Fort Souville.

12 July   German forces reach Fort Souville – the furthest point of the advance on Verdun – but are repelled.

4 September   Disaster as fire sweeps the French-held railway tunnel at Tavannes.

19 October   French counter-offensive begins.

24 October   Fort Douaumont is retaken. Mangin's forces recover in one day what it had taken the Germans four-and-a-half months to capture.

2 November   Fort Vaux is retaken.

18 November   The Battle of the Somme ends.

12 December   The German Chancellor offers to open peace negotiations with the Entente countries.

15 December   Launch of final French push on the right bank, aimed at pushing the German force back to the positions it held in February.

1917

April   Nivelle orchestrates French offensive at Chemin des Dames.

June   German forces overrun some right-bank positions during minor offensive operations ahead of Verdun.

August   French forces retake Mort Homme and Côte 304.

1918

Autumn   Joint American–French operation expels the last of the German force from the Verdun sector.

1

Verdun-sur-Meuse

Blindest of all, the blind who will not see.
On truth and fortitude outpour your hate.
With imperturbable tranquillity,
France hears the knocking at her Eastern gate.

Bathe here in blood the plumage of your pride;
Smite with your thunder till the ramparts nod;
Fools, who discern not, ere the gates fling wide,
The imminent whirlwind of the wrath of God.
H. L. Doak, *Verdun*

WHEN, AT A quarter-past seven on the morning of 21 February 1916, the German Fifth Army attacked the French fortress city of Verdun, a campaign of relentless terror was instigated. It would take some ten months, and the loss of over 700,000 lives, before the battle came to an end. Even by the brutal standards set by World War I, this was an incomparably long

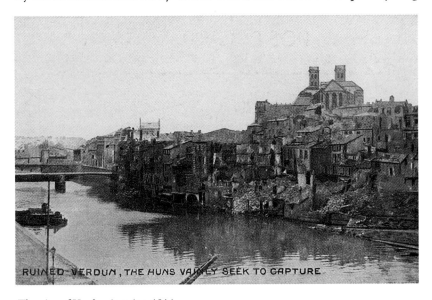

The city of Verdun in ruins, 1916.

and intense engagement, a merciless tragedy widely believed to represent a negation of centuries of civilized human development and progress. One French gunner noted from the battlefield how, it seemed to him, the world had 'gone back a thousand years'.

Yet, to many contemporary observers, there was a macabre logic to the location of the battle and to the protagonists involved. It made sense that the recent bitter rivalries of Germany and France should come to this, at a place imbued with a deep symbolic resonance for both sides, and which had previously served as the site of fighting between trans-Rhenish forces. Surely it was no small coincidence that Verdun should be the spot chosen for this most attritional of battles, in this the most attritional of wars.

Indeed, Verdun has had a chequered past, the 1916 battle being the most recent and brutal of ten hostile attacks to which the city has been subjected. The occurrence of such conflict was a result of more than just mere geography. The settlement had a strategic importance dating back to Roman times, when it was established as a notable stop on the roads from Metz to Reims and Paris. It had an equally important military significance, with the local landscape lending itself to fortification. Over the centuries, human endeavours compounded these natural lineaments in the Verdun area and, from 1624, the city itself was fortressed with the building of the vast citadel. In consequence, Verdun became a defensive position of some greatness. That fact, however, made it all the more desirable to invading forces.

Then there was the distant political significance of the city, felt in Germany as well as in France. In AD 843, a treaty signed at Verdun divided the Carolingian empire between the discordant heirs of Charlemagne, giving expression for the first time to what might be termed a Germanic nation state. Simultaneously, the embryonic form of modern France emerged. Under the terms of the treaty, Verdun was annexed to the newly constituted kingdom of Lorraine and came under indirect French influence. In 923 the city passed into the Germanic empire. A period of bishopric rule came to an end in the thirteenth century and was followed by another longer period of Germanic tutelage. The town was eventually claimed for France in 1552 by King Henri II.

In 1792 Verdun was bombarded by Prussian forces during the French Revolutionary Wars. Anti-Republican sentiment within the town forced a capitulation, and Verdun was held for six weeks. It was only after the French victory at Valmy that the occupying army was forced to leave. In 1870, towards the end of the Franco-Prussian War, Verdun was again attacked but this time resistance was stiffer. A fierce siege and three separate bombardments of increasing severity finally forced a surrender, Verdun being the last of the major French fortresses to fold. The Meuse province, including Verdun, was subsequently commanded by a prefect called von Bethmann-Hollweg, father of the future wartime Chancellor of Germany.

For those alive to witness the 1916 battle, this last event would have been the most telling harbinger of what was to unfurl at Verdun that terrible year. For Franco-German rivalry, which was always keenly felt, heightened considerably after the war of 1870. Defeat at the hands of the Prussians had come as an unexpected and humiliating shock to the French. Going into the battle confidence could not have been higher. Military, political, and civilian opinion all revelled in perceived notions of the French Army's invincibility. The fact that such mythical ideas – which owed much to the era of Napoleon's First Empire – manifested themselves at a time when France was militarily, diplomatically, and politically vulnerable throughout Europe – largely as a result of recent Prussian manoeuvrings – did enough to mask the true reality of France's international standing and overall military strength.

Under conditions of such grand illusion, Franco-Prussian relations had simmered for some years, following Bismarck's humiliation of the Emperor Napoleon III in 1866, when he secured the latter's neutrality for the duration of the Austro-Prussian War. Under false pretences, the Emperor was offered a notional territorial recompense along the Rhine. Before the issue could be addressed, however, Bismarck sued for a peace that excluded the French. Thereafter, anti-Prussian sentiment took something of a hold within certain circles of influence in Paris, but Napoleon III – who was suffering from ill-health and declining domestic prestige – failed to act against the new Prussian menace.

Crisis point was reached in 1870 over the proposed Hohenzollern candidacy to the vacant Spanish throne. French opposition to Prussia extending its control directly upon Spain – a country considered to fall into their sphere of influence – was vociferous, and enough to force a withdrawal of the application to fill the throne. Bismarck, however, seemed to be bent on confrontation with the French as a means of consolidating his emerging nation. He managed to manipulate this rare French diplomatic victory to his advantage by re-editing the Ems telegram in a manner that suggested the King of Prussia had snubbed the French ambassador to Berlin when he requested assurances that the candidacy would not be renewed at a later date. Opinion in France was outraged and the demand for retributive action – as a means of restoring national pride – widespread. The forces of both nations mobilized and, on 19 July 1870, war was declared.

The French Army was totally unprepared for combat, a situation the Prussians exploited by immediately taking the offensive initiative. In terms of troop numbers and weapon technology Prussia had superiority, and employed tactics to which the bungling French had no answer. A series of quick reverses in early August swung the battle decisively in Prussia's favour, and culminated in France losing all of the province of Alsace and a large part of Lorraine. General Bazaine, who took overall command of French forces from the ailing Emperor, withdrew to Metz where he immediately became encircled. The Emperor then re-entered the fray, raising a fresh army in the forlorn hope of relieving Metz. This force became engulfed at Sedan. After a period of some resistance there – during which time the Prussians inflicted heavy losses on the French – the Emperor surrendered with some 100,000 men, on 1 September. The war had barely entered its sixth week. Capitulation at Metz swiftly followed and the Second Empire was simply swept away. The Republic which replaced it overwhelmingly favoured the negotiation of a peace settlement.

The Treaty of Frankfurt, confirming France's humiliation at the hands of the Prussians, was signed in May 1871. Under the terms of the treaty, Prussia retained all conquered territories in Alsace and Lorraine, and levied upon the vanquished a massive indemnity of some 5 billion francs, with an army of occupation to be billeted in eastern France until this was paid in full. At a stroke France had lost 1,500,000 people to the new German empire – which had been proclaimed on French soil at Versailles – and an area of immense industrial and strategic importance.

Nevertheless, France bounced back from the nadir of 1870 in a relatively short time. The reparations – funded largely through foreign loans – were paid as early as 1873. A period of economic and social renaissance followed though, politically, matters were less assured as the new Republic took time firmly to establish itself. Military reforms were intensified and went hand in hand with the construction of a heavy defensive system of fortifications in the east of the country. Stretching in a line from the Belgian frontier in the north to Belfort in the south, this system was designed to shield France from German aggression, and allow the country – in the event of an attack from the east – to be able to mobilize its forces effectively. Verdun was integral to this line of defence and was built up to become one of, if not the most, heavily fortified areas along the new border. Thus, from a French point of view, the city's significance became popularly intertwined with the symbolic and vexing issue of Alsace-Lorraine.

Bismarck remained aware of the fact that the French would, given the chance, attempt to reclaim the land lost in 1870. Despite the contentiousness attached to the disputed provinces, however, the German Chancellor remained committed to holding on to his country's territorial spoils;

not only did they bolster Germany's border against a possible resurgent France, they were also a rich source of natural raw materials. Until his removal from power in 1890, it was to this end that Bismarck tailored much of his foreign policy, devoting considerable time and effort to keeping France diplomatically isolated and weak in terms of its international status.

At the same time, around the turn of the century, French public and political opinion was being consistently deflected from the entire Alsace-Lorraine question by a variety of issues, such as empire-building in Africa and, at home, the Dreyfus Affair. Nevertheless, the desire for some kind of punitive strike against Germany was never far from the surface of French society during this time (though one must be careful not to make the mistake of overestimating the effectiveness of this body of opinion, which rarely had the *materiel* – let alone the opportunity – practically to change the status quo). The *revanchists*, who epitomized this tendency, wished to see at the very least the return to France of Alsace-Lorraine, and such feeling was especially marked within the military establishment. Consequently, the Alsace question remained an issue of some contention in France prior to war in 1914. Indeed, in the years immediately preceding the outbreak of hostilities, it once again moved forcefully to the top of the French domestic political agenda. And especially so in 1911 after the blundering attempted intervention at Agadir by the Germans, when an international incident was averted only by British mediation and some desperate last-minute negotiating.

During the latter stages of the July Crisis of 1914, when Europe's precarious alliance system was bringing the continent daily closer to the brink of catastrophe, the German Chancellor, Theobald von Bethmann-Hollweg, contacted his counterparts in Paris and St Petersburg. To the Russians he sent an ultimatum demanding that they terminate all perceived aggressive measures within twelve hours. Simultaneously, Russia's ally, France, was required to pledge within eighteen hours to remain neutral in any ensuing conflict should Russia refuse to acquiesce to this demand. Further, the French were asked to hand over to Germany possession of the fortifications at Verdun and Toul as a means of guaranteeing this neutrality. The day after the ultimatum was issued, 1 August, Russia and Germany were at war, and France ordered the general mobilization of its forces.

Germany and France each mobilized with great efficiency. More than 2,000,000 French and 1,500,000 German troops were brought effectively into service in a matter of days. These two considerable forces were literally to crash into one another as both countries pursued blueprints for war that had been prepared years in advance for just such a confrontation.

The French war plan, known as Plan XVII, was disastrously negated by the intense German barrage that their forces met almost everywhere. The idea behind the plan was relatively straightforward, allowing for four of France's five armies to surge forward towards the Rhine, advancing through the disputed regions of Lorraine and Alsace. If needed, two of these armies could be diverted northwards into the Ardennes region to head off any German advances there. The entire objective depended on the Germans being taken by surprise. If the French succeeded in this aim, it was calculated, the enemy's mobilization plans – and by extension, their entire war effort – would be critically destabilized. The Germans, however, were far too well prepared to be caught out in such a manner and met the advancing French forces head on. In a calamitous two-week period, France lost around 300,000 men and nearly 5000 officers. The Germans, meanwhile, pursued relentlessly their predetermined war plan, which was so well rehearsed as almost to be cast in stone. It very nearly succeeded.

The Schlieffen Plan – named after the German Chief-of-Staff who devised it in 1891 – was framed as a means of allowing Germany to fight a war successfully on two fronts, an ever-increasing likelihood in the light of developing friendly relations between France and Russia (the two were to ratify a treaty of alliance in 1894). Essentially, Schlieffen developed a strategy that aimed to defeat France as speedily as possible, before the massive Russian military machine had time to mobilize effectively. In this way, it was hoped, Germany would have to fight actively at any one time on only a single front. The defeat of France was to be facilitated by an invasion of the country through neutral Belgium – a risk that was eventually to result in Britain's entry into the war – with the advancing army arching around and turning eastwards from a point on the lower Seine. It would then attack the fortified zone and French Army from the rear, sandwiching those forces between a holding army in Alsace-Lorraine. With the French encircled, it was believed, they could be readily crushed. The entire process was calculated to last no longer than six weeks, about the time it would take Russia fully to mobilize. Germany could then focus the bulk of its forces in an easterly direction.

In the event, the Germans progressed through Belgium and into northern France relatively unhindered and with some rapidity. The plan started to falter only as a result of a tactical error of judgement made by the German Chief-of-Staff, General Count von Moltke. The holding off of the Russians in eastern Prussia proved to be more difficult than expected and the operation required urgent reinforcement. But rather than transferring troops from the less vulnerable First Army which was situated in comparative safety in Lorraine, Moltke diverted men from the hastening Second Army in northern France. Then, instead of advancing on Paris when it was a matter of some 45 kilometres from the capital city, the Second Army was directed towards eastern France as a means of speeding up the defeat of the French there.

As it pushed across the Marne region, French forces – supported by the British Expeditionary Force – attacked the German Second Army on 5 September, exploiting the gaps that existed between the positions of various German divisions. The latter were subsequently compelled to retreat across the River Aisne in the direction from which they had entered France, and a decisive victory was won for the Entente powers. The cost in purely human terms, however, was high. Nevertheless, the Schlieffen Plan had been defeated. France was thereafter able to establish and to hold a tenable position and consequently could not be readily knocked out of the war. Germany, on the other hand, was now destined to do what its military planners had hoped to avoid – fight the war on two fronts simultaneously.

Thereafter, both sides fell back and stood their ground. During the ensuing weeks and months, a front – running from the Swiss border to the Belgian coast – was established as continuous lines of opposing trenches were excavated. The short war, which so many had predicted and planned for, was developing into a protracted affair that clearly was going to last considerably longer than expected.

The fortifications at Verdun had played their part in blocking the German Army in 1914, and the region was enveloped in a dense defensive network of fortifications causing the Western Front to become instituted *around* the bulwarked area, forming a prominent salient jutting into the German line. Subsequently, the region settled down and, in the light of what was to come, took on a peculiarly quiet air. In the words of one contemporary French observer, the city became 'simply a town behind the front, where officers and men congregated in their hours of leave, and tried to forget the trials and horrors of the trenches'.

The year 1915 was to see no considerable changes anywhere along the Western Front. All attempts to break through ended in heavy casualties for little or no gain. In April, the Germans took the initiative at Ypres, almost breaking through with their novel, yet under developed, weapon of gas. Thereafter, they remained on a defensive footing along the whole of the front in the west. France spearheaded all allied operations throughout the year, attempting to unhinge the Germans and drive through their line by forcing them out into the open. Neither at Artois in May, nor at Champagne in September, did the tactic succeed. The Germans steadfastly refused to be drawn out and, despite all endeavours, could not be driven out. The year was a highly wasteful one in terms of human life and tangible achievement, and ended in absolute stalemate with both sides resolutely holding the line.

In the midst of all this, a pattern was beginning to emerge, within which human life was expendable. The French Commander-in-Chief, Joseph Joffre, gave expression to this in an Order of the Day, issued on 7 September 1915, which stated: 'Troops who can no longer advance must at all costs keep the ground they have conquered or die on the spot rather than give way. In the present circumstances, no faltering can be tolerated.' Such sentiment was to resonate heavily at Verdun in 1916.

2

Prelude to Combat

The world bloodily-minded,
The Church dead or polluted,
The blind leading the blinded,
And the deaf dragging the muted.
Israel Zangwill, 1916.

VICTORY AT THE Marne in September 1914 proved to be the French
Commander-in-Chief Joffre's greatest military success. Wittingly or
unwittingly – and there is some disagreement among historians over the
point – he had pulled matters back from the brink of disaster and saved
France from an ignominious and early defeat by handling a fraught situation with charismatic calm. It was to be the high point of his career.
Subsequently, his star began to wane. This resulted largely from the fact
that Joffre had no viable alternative strategy in reserve for pursuing the
war effort and breaking the deadlock along the Western Front.

Throughout 1915 Joffre was responsible for the severe haemorrhaging
of life from the rank and file of the French Army for negligible returns.
Mounting political criticism – which was compounded by Joffre's often
blatant disregard for opinion that emanated from France's National
Assembly – could be shrugged off only for so long.

By December 1915, the government had forced the selection of
General de Castlenau as Joffre's right-hand man. His remit was to rein in
the Commander-in-Chief. The appointment represented an immense
squandering of power by Joffre. In the aftermath of the Marne success, the
Grand Quartier Général – the nerve centre of the French Command which
was headed by Joffre – had considerable authority and was, in the absence
of a government (which had temporarily fled from Paris for the relative
tranquillity of Bordeaux) to assume overall and direct responsibility for
the conduct of the war.

Joseph Jacques Césaire Joffre was born in the Pyrenées region of south-
western France on 12 January 1852. He trained for military life at the
École Polytechnique in Paris, interrupting his studies in 1870 and 1871 to
serve as a junior officer in the defence of Paris during the Franco-Prussian

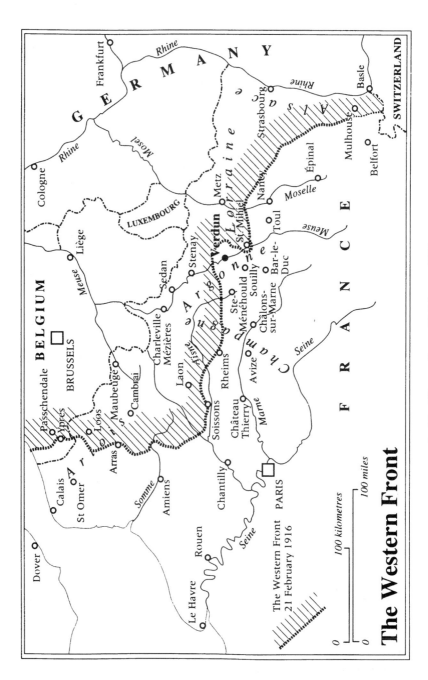

1   The Western Front, 21 February 1916

War. After completing his training, he entered the army and served as an engineer in France until 1885. He then requested a transfer to the colonial services and spent the next fifteen years in various parts of the French empire – Indo-China, western Africa, and Madagascar. During this time he established for himself something of a reputation as an expert in his specialized field, largely as a result of his work on fortifications in Madagascar. In 1894 he achieved a degree of notoriety after he successfully led an expedition to Timbuktu. At this time, however, his name remained little known outside of French military circles.

Joffre returned to France in 1900 and, within five years, had been promoted to the rank of Major-General. A year later he took command of an infantry division and then a Corps. By 1910 he was a member of the Supreme War Council with specific responsibilities for war planning. In July 1911 he was the surprise choice for the elevated position of Chief of the General Staff. The appointment was unexpected largely because Joffre – never renowned as a great intellect – did not have the considered relevant training for the post, nor did he have much practical combat experience. Conversely, though, there were other factors working in his favour. He was fifty-nine years old, young enough to be expected to last in the job for some time. More importantly perhaps, he was politically clean. He had been out of France for much of the Dreyfus case, for example, and so was not tainted in the same manner as many of his peers. Nor did he have any obvious religious affiliations – a major hindrance to promotion in the avowedly Republican ranks of the French Army at this time. Arguably, then, his advance to the top had more to do with merit and certainly little to do with connection. He was humble enough, too, to recognize his shortcomings when accepting the job and applied for assistance from those most qualified to give it.

Between 1911 and the outbreak of the war, Joffre concentrated on the development of Plan XVII. He also oversaw the upgrading of France's defensive positions and, crucially, framed the 1913 Conscription Bill which saw the reintroduction of a minimum three-year period of military service. Joffre was not – nor did he claim to be – a brilliant military man. He was a mediocre strategist and tactician whose great strength was his ability to comprehend the widest of pictures with equal measures of detachment and assuredness. His lack of nerves and cool manner were renowned, and in the darkest days of 1914 are said to have soothed the concerns of many a French Army commander. It was during this time that his reputation as a 'man from the people and of the people, plain in character as in origin' was cemented. The fact that he did not buckle in the earliest days of the war when Plan XVII began to unravel, coupled with his eternal confidence and contagious optimism – which, as time was to

Guerre de 1914
Le Général JOFFRE

General Joffre, Commander-in-Chief of French forces, 1916

show, were often gravely misplaced – all added to his allure, and a certain mystique attached itself to him. His regular habits merely compounded his image as a formidable character: he was a hearty eater, which was reflected in his portly stature, and slept long and regular hours from which he was famously never disturbed. Later, during the Battle of Verdun, he was to remain as unruffled as ever. Winston Churchill wrote that, throughout the crisis days of 1916, Joffre 'remained in Olympian tranquillity, inspiring by his unaffected calm . . . confidence in all about him'.

The stalemate which characterized the Western Front throughout late 1914 and the whole of 1915 gave rise to a certain amount of impatience among the governments of the leading protagonists of the war. They were becoming ever more anxious at the high material and human costs of the campaign. Leaders on both sides were keen to force some kind of breakthrough in the west. The fact that the leading commanders of all the main armies desired the same pointed to 1916 being the year when the deadlock might finally be broken.

Among the Entente Powers, most leading commanders – who, up to this point, had failed to act in a wholly concerted manner – believed that the war would ultimately be won or lost on the Western Front. They agreed, however, that it was essential that the pressure be kept up on the Central Powers on all fronts. To this end, on 6 December 1915 at Joffre's headquarters at Chantilly, the allied powers held their first joint military conference.

In terms of decisive planning, discussions were at best vague but a general scheme was hatched for simultaneous offensive actions against Germany and its allies on all fronts. The leading lights at the conference, Joffre and the newly appointed Commander-in-Chief of British forces in France and Flanders, Field Marshal Sir Douglas Haig, were both avid exponents of the offensive, and decided to put this philosophical tendency into practice as soon as circumstances allowed. The Italians were not considered truly formidable enough to mount the sort of campaign that would keep the Central states occupied for long, and Russia was already destabilized by a worsening domestic situation. It was immediately clear, therefore, that the mainstay of the general allied offensive plans for 1916 would rest with a joint Franco-British attack against the Germans in the west. With the British Army in France rapidly expanding in size, this truly represented the best chance of achieving a breakthrough that would, it was hoped, act as a precursor for successes elsewhere.

The choice for the location of this attack was the strangely insignificant one – from a strategic point of view – of the Somme. It was chosen simply because it was the point on the map at which British and French forces met and thus was where it could be expected that the greatest losses could be inflicted on the German forces for the minimal effort. This reality notwithstanding, there was no other reward to be claimed at this spot. As A. J. P. Taylor noted: 'The Germans, if pressed [at the Somme], could fall back to their own advantage, with better communications and a shortened line.'

Before the ink on the plan had a chance to dry, however, the Germans pre-empted the Franco-British initiative by striking against the French at Verdun. This was an exceptional move, for it represented the only time between the Marne in 1914 and the offensive actions of March and April 1918 – Ypres notwithstanding – that the Germans abandoned a defensive position on the Western Front. Verdun, then, was to be the only major deviation from a trusted strategy that allowed the allies, at great cost, to throw attack after attack at a seemingly inviolable line. The mastermind of the offensive against Verdun – who, like his counterparts Joffre and Haig, believed that the war would be decisively settled in the west – was the German Chief of the General Staff, Erich von Falkenhayn.

Details of Falkenhayn's formative years are, at best, sketchy. He was born on 11 September 1861 near Thorn in western Prussia. His Junker estate-owning family had fallen on hard times and sent their son at an early age to Cadet School. He graduated to the War Academy, passing through with distinction – he was third in his class – in 1890. Then, in 1896, he

General von Falkenhayn, German Chief of the General Staff,
1916, mastermind of the attack on Verdun

travelled to China as captain of an expeditionary corps, staying on as a
major and taking up the post of instructor at the Chinese Military School.
As a staff officer, he was to assist in the quelling of the Boxer Rebellion in
1899.

Reports of Falkenhayn's time in the Far East were most favourable,
making a positive impression upon his superiors in Germany and thereby
facilitating a rapid rise through the ranks of the German military. He
became a Lieutenant-Colonel in 1905, a Colonel in 1908, and, three
years later, commander of a guard. Thereafter, he passed through the rank
of Major-General before his appointment in July 1913 as Prussian War
Minister. He was fifty-one years old.

The outbreak of World War I, and the wrecking of the Schlieffen Plan
on the Marne in September 1914, further facilitated Falkenhayn's ascendancy when he was called upon to replace the disgraced Chief of the
General Staff, von Moltke. For a short time, he continued to combine this
post with that of Prussian War Minister, the first time that this had

General Count von Moltke, German Chief of the General
Staff at the outbreak of World War I

happened. His speedy elevation led, almost inevitably, to Falkenhayn developing a reputation for being an unashamed careerist. Something of a traditionalist in outlook – he advocated the right to duelling, for example, and upheld the traditional notion of an officer's honour – he was clever and ruthless in his dealings with others. His intellectual capacities and insight were respected and looked to during the early months of the war, though never rigorously tested.

Falkenhayn's manner was aloof, however, and, in his dealings with others, he conveyed a lack of human warmth. He gave off the air of one who was precise in action and quick witted in thought. In reality, though, he tended to act in a strangely indecisive manner when it mattered most. At Verdun, on a number of crucial occasions, he failed to press home a military advantage when that is precisely what circumstances required. Undeniably, he tended to err on the side of caution throughout World War I, possibly as a result of the expensive failure to break through at Ypres in the spring of 1915. Nonetheless, this was a somewhat paradoxical trait for a military general who believed that the decisive action of the war was destined to occur on the Western Front. He was undoubtedly encumbered in his ability to act decisively in the west, however, for he was continually forced to balance Germany's armies, artillery, and war materials in a manner designed to allow the Central Powers successfully to pursue a war on two major fronts. In the event, he had neither the personal nor practical capacities for overseeing such an operation.

Nevertheless, Falkenhayn believed that the prosecution of a strategy of attrition could yield dividends along the static Western Front, and this was to influence utterly his decision to attack French forces at Verdun in 1916. Some nine days after the allied commanders had met at Chantilly, Falkenhayn was outlining his analysis of the general situation facing Germany and its allies at the end of 1915, and setting out his proposals for action the following year in a famous memorandum to the Kaiser, Wilhelm II. Taking the widest possible view of matters as they stood, he concluded that Germany's prime foe in the war was none other than Britain. He warned the Kaiser: 'The history of the English wars against the Netherlands, Spain, France and Napoleon is being repeated. Germany can expect no mercy [from Britain]'. He concluded, therefore, that some kind of heavy blow needed to be made against the prime enemy from across the North Sea. But he also cautioned that Germany could no longer afford to maintain a largely defensive posture, for it would ultimately be crushed by the superior resources that would soon be made available to the combined allied forces. He wrote: 'Our enemies . . . are increasing their resources much more than we are. If that process continues a moment must come when the balance of numbers itself will deprive Germany of all remaining hope.'

The warning was a stark one, made all the more potent by its irresistible logic. The likelihood of staving off the inevitable, however, by striking a decisive or mortal blow against the British presented problems of almost insurmountable proportions. The only means available to the Germans for directly striking a blow against the British was via a formidable and indiscriminate campaign of submarine warfare. This would aim at cutting off Britain's supply and trade routes with its empire, thus destabilizing the war effort and starving the island's population into submission. Falkenhayn favoured such a strategy but was only too well aware that it was unlikely to find favour among German political circles – least of all with the Kaiser. It was widely (and in the event, correctly) assumed that such a campaign was likely to embroil the United States of America in the more general conflict. Nevertheless, Falkenhayn noted that:

Submarine warfare strikes at the enemy's most sensitive spot, because it aims at severing his oversea communications . . . [If] unrestricted submarine war must force England to yield in the course of the year 1916 . . . we must face the fact that the United States may take up a hostile attitude.

Returning to the European arena of the war, Falkenhayn underlined the fact that, owing to a number of factors – available resources in terms of men and artillery, the lie of the land in strategic and geographical senses – there were no reasonable practical grounds for believing that Germany could succeed in an all-out offensive anywhere along the Western Front. He believed, however – and this was the crux of the issue – that Britain was never destined to play more than a minor part in the war in continental Europe because of the comparative weakness of its land forces. He observed, 'for England the campaign on the Continent of Europe with her own troops is at bottom a side-show'. And he concluded that, to this end, 'Her real weapons here [that is, on continental Europe] are the French, Russian and Italian Armies.' If these could each be knocked out of the war – or at the least, debilitated to the point where their continued participation became an irrelevance – Falkenhayn argued that Britain's ability to pursue the war, along with its 'lust for our destruction', would ultimately be brought to an end.

He dismissed the Italian Army almost out of hand as being little more than an irrelevance to be dealt with at some point in the future by the armies of the Austro-Hungarian empire. With regard to Russia, Falkenhayn believed that 'internal troubles will compel her to give in' sooner rather than later but that, nevertheless, a German advance on the Eastern Front was a big gamble, the risks involved being so large as to render such a move unjustifiable. 'There remains only France', he continued.

As I have already insisted, the strain on France has almost reached breaking point – though it is certainly borne with the most remarkable devotion. If we succeeded in opening the eyes of her people to the fact that in a military sense they have nothing more to hope for . . . breaking point would be reached and England's best sword knocked out of her hand. To achieve that object the uncertain method of a mass break-through [against France], in any case beyond our means, is unnecessary. We can probably do enough for our purposes with limited resources. Within our reach behind the French sector of the Western front there are objectives for the retention of which the French General Staff would be compelled to throw in every man they have. If they do so the forces of France will bleed to death – as there can be no question of a voluntary withdrawal – whether we reach our goal or not. If they do not do so, and we reach our objectives, the moral effect on France will be enormous. For an operation limited to a narrow front Germany will not be compelled to spend herself so completely that all other fronts are practically drained.

The plan was an ingenious one, albeit one with seemingly dual objectives, which showed a comprehensive understanding not only of the strategic and military situations as they stood, but also the psychological imperatives dictating the pursual of the war from a French point of view. The stated primary objective – of *bleeding* French forces to *death* – was chilling in its practical implications and in the removed coolness with which it was suggested. Alistair Horne has written that never before 'had any great commander or strategist proposed to vanquish an enemy by gradually bleeding him to death'. The bluntness of the suggestion and its macabre novelty were to win much support. Werner Beumelberg, one of the official German historians of the Battle of Verdun, revelled in the fact that Germany 'must apply a suction pump to the body of France, and gradually but steadily drain the strength from its half-open veins'.

The Kaiser immediately warmed to Falkenhayn's presentation. It appealed to him on a number of levels and for many reasons, especially once the location for the operation – it had been a straightforward choice between Belfort and Verdun – was decided. This meant that the Kaiser's son, the Crown Prince Wilhelm, would lead his Fifth Army in what

The German High Command, 1914–18. The Crown Prince is standing fourth from left; Falkenhayn, seventh from left. Seated is the Kaiser, Wilhelm II, fourth from left; Hindenburg, eighth from the left

might possibly turn out to be one of the decisive – and, therefore, most glorious – campaigns of the war. Furthermore, the anti-British sentiment that ran throughout the entire memorandum was undoubtedly deliberate, for it played up to the Kaiser's own prejudices (he had little time for his British blood relations). Moreover, the fact that the plan offered an apparently genuine chance of achieving a viable breakthrough further combined to guarantee Wilhelm II's approval for the suggested offensive.

It was decided, then, that France's military forces were to be ensnared at Verdun, for it had been calculated that the French commanding staff would defend this symbolically important defensive link to the hilt, regardless of its actual significance or the costs, until their forces were drained of all life. As Churchill surmised in *The World Crisis*:

> Verdun was to become an anvil upon which French military manhood was to be hammered to death by German cannon. The French were to be fastened to fixed positions by sentiment, and battered to pieces there by artillery.

It was predicted that, thereafter, with France defeated, Russia would be forced to sue for an early peace ahead of impending domestic implosion because its forces would be unable to cope with such internal turmoil and a concentrated German attack along the Eastern Front. Britain would then be left isolated and unable to continue the war alone against the marauding Central Powers.

In the event, however, the proposal to turn Verdun into an anvil was not made abundantly clear to all those who were involved practically in undertaking the operation. There was some confusion about what the ultimate objective to be attained at Verdun was. Indeed, Falkenhayn had deliberately left the plan shrouded in ambiguity. The Crown Prince, for example, who was to command the onslaught upon Verdun – and who, after the event, admitted to finding 'something uncommonly attractive' about Falkenhayn's memorandum to his father – believed that he had been set the definite objective of capturing the fortress of Verdun itself. Under the terms of Falkenhayn's strategy, however, this was undeniably a secondary aim. He wished merely to debilitate fatally France's forces at Verdun by forcing them into a deadly war of attrition in defence of this most symbolically potent of cities. If Verdun fell before this objective could be achieved, then the entire process of *bleeding* could not take place.

If the bleeding process was not allowed the opportunity to take place, however – if the French were to capitulate at Verdun – all would not be lost for the Germans. As Falkenhayn observed in his memorandum, the loss of Verdun would have a 'moral effect on France [that] will be enormous'. He was obviously hedging his bets to some extent, though he fully believed that Verdun would not fall without the mightiest of struggles. In a practical sense, the capture of Verdun would, to some small degree, strengthen the German line in the west. It would also serve to bolster morale within the ranks of the German Army, and boost public opinion at home which was beginning to feel the pinch as the war entered its third calendar year. In some respects, therefore, the fact that the plan had a dual objective – which served to confuse matters with regard to the *true* purpose of the exercise – also happened to guarantee, or so it was believed, some sort of success for the Germans on the Western Front in 1916. As the military historian John Keegan has commented of Falkenhayn's strategy: 'If the French gave up the struggle, they would lose Verdun; if they persisted, they would lose their army'. Either way, Falkenhayn could not envisage an outcome by which Germany ended up in a worse situation, either from a military or a strategic viewpoint.

It has been suggested of Falkenhayn that he was something of an opportunist so far as his scheme for attacking at Verdun in 1916 was concerned. The point is a fair one. There can be little doubt, however, that, given the choice, he would sooner have seen France broken militarily than the fortifications at Verdun fall into German hands. Indeed, the former occurrence would merely facilitate the latter. It is quite possible that he did not advertise his real intentions regarding Verdun because to do so might have had a negative effect on those officers and troops who were being asked to perform the task of bleeding the French Army. No soldiers go into battle in a confident mood if they do not feel that the stated objective is clearly defined and, moreover, readily attainable. A military commander is even less likely to perform to the best of his abilities if he believes his task is simply to become involved in a war of attrition.

Unknown to Falkenhayn, when he was originating his strategy for an offensive on Verdun, the fortresses' military importance had been considerably undermined by the previous actions of Joffre. Although in military and civilian circles it was still widely assumed to be inviolable, in fact, by the beginning of 1916, Verdun and its environs had been largely disarmed. All substantial, moveable weaponry had been removed to elsewhere on the front – Artois, Champagne – to facilitate other operations. Moreover, in the light of the form the Western Front now took, the fortresses' wider strategic significance was not actually as great as many thought. Of course, this fact *would* have entered the German Chief of Staff's calculations, and brings further into focus his real intentions regarding Verdun.

Once assent had been given for the attack, German preparations for the battle were carried out efficiently, with total thoroughness, and in almost complete secrecy. Nothing was to be overlooked and every attention was paid to the smallest of details. Falkenhayn later reminisced that, in the weeks immediately prior to engagement at Verdun, 'every demand for labour and equipment was complied with'. The operation was unique in its nature and in its scale. An entire army corps was transported to the region directly behind the German line facing Verdun to assist in preparation for the attack. An entire military settlement, comprising all the necessary materials for servicing large numbers of troops, was established within striking distance of the French position. Here was to be the convergence point for German soldiers who would travel to fight at Verdun from all parts of the general battle area within control of the Central Powers.

Before the combat infantry and artillery arrived, whole areas – including villages, farms, and other settlements – were evacuated of civilians, and property requisitioned, to make way for this vast army, its equipment, guns, and ammunition, which were to be so heavily concentrated in the area. Kilometres of telephone and communications lines had to be laid and trenches dug. Rations and ammunition – enough for some weeks – were brought to the front line and stored under protective shell-proof and weather-resistant covers. Entire batteries were brilliantly camouflaged by enormous drapes to ensure they were not spotted from the air by French intelligence sources. Ten new railway lines, and some twenty or more new rail stations, had to be built to facilitate the moving of so much human and material resource into such a geographically restricted zone, a zone that stretched the few densely wooded kilometres from the foothills of the Meuse to the German front line.

Vast underground hideaways, or *Stollen*, were constructed deep into the Earth's surface at no small human effort, to keep the German soldiers safely out of the view of the enemy. These subterranean barracks could reach variously between 4.5 and 14 metres deep, and consequently, were perfectly immune from the best efforts of enemy artillery bombardment. They were massive structures, too. The *Stollen* at the woods of Consenvoye – which was about 900 metres or so from the forward French line – could hold anything up to 1200 men. In a moment of sheer folly, the French General Staff, whose intelligence sources could hardly fail to notice the digging of such momentous burrows, chose to decree that the *Stollen* were being built simply to serve a defensive purpose, and should not therefore be considered to be of much concern. Consequently, reports about the building of the *Stollen*, which started to filter back to the French from early January 1916, had little significance attached to them.

Despite the best efforts of the French intelligence services and listening posts operating in the Verdun region – which worked as well as circumstances would allow and which continually managed to gain odd, yet important, strands of information about German activities close to the French front line – no one in a position of authority at French general headquarters immediately acted upon this information nor drew the obvious inference that something rather serious was being planned by the Germans. In this respect, the French remained blind to what was going on in front of them until the last minute, indeed, until it was almost too late.

Strangely, this was also true for many of those who were politically and militarily aligned with the attacking forces. Falkenhayn, it would seem, was an exceptionally secretive character who was – perhaps rightly – excessively worried about the leaking of information to the enemy. Prior to the offensive at Verdun, therefore, he was keen not to share his plans with anyone other than those directly involved in the operation. Consequently, knowledge of what had become known as Operation *Gericht* – variously translated as meaning 'Scaffold' or 'Place of Execution' – was not common even throughout the upper echelons of the German Army. As late as 7 January 1916 – when the vast movement of men and machinery towards and around the Western Front made it obvious even to the most unobservant of officers that a rather large offensive was imminent somewhere along the line – Falkenhayn was claiming that he was yet to finalize the eventual point of attack. It was not just fellow German commanders who were left in the dark by the Chief of the General Staff. The government at Berlin, and the Chancellor Bethmann-Hollweg, were not privy to knowledge of the plan until immediately before its execution. Even more surprisingly, perhaps, Falkenhayn failed to inform his prime ally, Austria-Hungary, and its Commander-in-Chief, Field Marshal Conrad von Hötzendorf, of the impending offensive.

Falkenhayn, then, was apparently happy to undertake one of the Central Powers' principal offensive operations of the entire war in utter isolation and total secrecy. In so doing, he infuriated a number of important allies and colleagues. In the longer term, this was to backfire with drastic consequences for the entire assault on Verdun. In the shorter term, it was the first example, of many, of the General acting in a taciturn manner. Throughout the campaign at Verdun he behaved with the utmost reticence, and kept a tight rein on matters, for the most part overseeing directly all aspects of battle tactics and strategy. Meanwhile, news of the impending attack spread only slowly and after publication of the official plans in late January. In short, these stated that an offensive upon the fortress of Verdun was to take place on 12 February 1916. It was to be limited in scope, and concentrated on the eastern, or right, bank of the Meuse approaching the city.

Before World War I, popular belief held that the fortress of Verdun could never be captured. French military propagandists told anyone who was prepared to listen that the line of defensive fortifications which converged upon Verdun could not be violated under any circumstances. No one had any reason to disbelieve such information. After all, available evidence suggested that Verdun's reputation, as one of the strongest fortifications in the world, was fully justified. When the occasion required it, some army generals and Deputies to the National Assembly even spoke of Verdun as being the strongest fortress anywhere on the planet. Events in 1914 and 1915 further enhanced this reputation. The fortress had stood up well to numerous assaults upon it, of varying intensity, by the German military throughout the formative stages of the war. Furthermore, it had functioned as a vital strategic pivot during the desperate rearguard actions of September 1914, when the French forces had managed to stave off an early defeat on the Marne.

All of this, however, merely disguised the fact that Verdun's defences had been severely neglected, to the point of being deliberately run down. Indeed, in such small regard was Verdun viewed by the French chief Joffre immediately before he launched the offensive action at the Marne, he actually ordered that the stronghold be abandoned. Fortunately for France, it was not, owing to the foresight shown by a locally based general, Sarrail, who blatantly ignored the command. Without Verdun there would have been no tangibly adequate block on a German advance westwards, through Lorraine and towards Paris.

Nevertheless, this apparently small yet necessary feat did little either to enamour Verdun and its fortifications to Joffre, nor convince him that it was an area likely to be pin-pointed by the Germans as a viable location for a concerted offensive action. Consequently, those heavy calibre guns (together with machine guns) which were characteristic of – and, indeed, integral to – the fortifications of the Verdun system, and which could be moved, were dismantled and taken elsewhere. Similarly, the garrisons attached to the region's forts, and billeted in the town, were also diverted away from duty at Verdun, in the belief that they could be put to better and more effective use elsewhere. By 1915, then, most of Verdun's garrison and the bulk of its artillery (some forty-three heavy batteries had been removed from the area by October 1915) were taken north and utilized during the Champagne offensive.

From a contemporaneous military viewpoint, there were justifiable reasons why the Verdun sector was down graded in this way. After the

German heavy artillery had virtually annihilated the Belgian fortresses at Liège and elsewhere in the opening moves of the war, the belief spread among the French command that fortifications were a dangerous liability that acted merely as a magnet, attracting deadly concentrations of enemy shell fire. As such, they were viewed with increasing suspicion, as death-traps best avoided, whose strategic disadvantages far outweighed any advantages. Furthermore, so far as Verdun itself was concerned, by the middle of 1915, the area had settled down into a relatively quiet sector, so quiet in fact, that Joffre no longer felt able to justify the expense of maintaining the fortress fully armed, when men and materials were in such short supply elsewhere along the front.

As a result, in August 1915 the down grading of the Verdun region was made official. Subsequently, the city's strategic and military significance was lessened, with the absorption of the Verdun system of fortifications into the newly created *Région Fortifée du Verdun* [Fortified Region of Verdun; hereafter, RFV]. This wartime bureaucratic-strategic domain was of considerable size, reaching from St Mihiel to the south-west of the city of Verdun, west to Avocourt, incorporating the entirety of the Verdun area. The new commander of the RFV, General Herr, had under his jurisdiction over 70 kilometres of front line.

In the context of the course the war in the west had taken in its first year, such reclassifying and down grading were, perhaps, understandable. The fact that the infantry and artillery placed at Verdun could be actively employed elsewhere along the front, fully justified their removal, provided it was stipulated that they could be redeployed to their place of origin if need be. Unfortunately, no such proviso existed, possibly because, as already mentioned, Verdun was considered to be a 'safe' zone despite its proximity to the German line.

Furthermore, the down grading was undertaken with little foresight as to the consequences of the action. For example, there was no concurrent realignment of the region's remaining defences to make them as invulnerable to capture as possible. The defensive apparatuses that were left in a weakened state, such as individual fortresses, were further left exposed to attack, because no new defensive trenches were dug before them. Nor was any effort made to upgrade lines of communication which were the only reliable link between the various forts in the area north of Verdun and the city itself. Moreover, the quality of troops transferred to Verdun, after its down grading but prior to the German offensive (mostly over-aged reservists who, under normal circumstances, would not have seen active combat duty), left something to be desired because they lacked vitality and strength. In the event of a sudden attack, these men could not be expected to offer much in the way of resistance to defend the positions they occupied.

In terms of France's ability to defend the point, the situation around Verdun in early 1916 was precarious to say the least. There existed insufficient weapons of high calibre, inadequate numbers of battle-ready troops, no tenable secondary defences (such as trenches), and few viable lines of communication. Those defences that were in place were either unserviced or largely cosmetic, consisting of rows of barbed wiring and the like, which served no practical shielding purposes.

As we have seen, the French Army hierarchy largely disregarded intelligence information regarding the build up of German activity before Verdun in early January 1916. Even when deserters started crossing the line to the French side – some warning that 'something terrible' was astir – the French General Staff was sluggish in its response. Slowly, and in an uneven and half-hearted manner, reservists were sent to work on a number of tasks, such as digging a defensible line to the north of the city on the right bank of the River Meuse. New defensive works were also started, though not finished, on the less-vulnerable left bank. None of this labour was carried out to a high enough standard, however.

So, in practical terms, Verdun was possibly one of the weakest links in the allied line along the Western Front. This should not have been the case, and few believed that it was. On taking command of the RFV in the late summer of 1915, General Herr undertook a comprehensive survey of the region in his charge, and was shocked by the implications of the results. He immediately set about trying to highlight to his superiors the vulnerable plight of the sector and the catastrophic potential which this represented. But no one seemed particularly interested or overly concerned. Too much was going on elsewhere to make a 'quiet' sector of any great concern, let alone one that was in no immediate danger. Each and every request Herr made for more men to carry out vital works was met with the same response: *no spare men are available, the necessary work can wait.* Until virtually the very eve of the proposed date for the German attack, Joffre continued to believe that: 'From the point of view of German strategy, Verdun has no justification'. It was in just such an atmosphere that, for months, Herr had been making exhortations to the *Grand Quartier Général* calling for affirmative action.

Another source, warning of the calamities that might befall the Verdun zone, was to emerge during 1915. Lieutenant-Colonel Emile Driant – who was to be killed at his post during the first days of the Battle of Verdun – had spent most of his life working as a professional soldier, using his experiences to pen a number of books on warfare. Apparently fed up at being continually passed over for promotion – allegedly because of his political connections – he left the French Army and entered the National Assembly as representative for a constituency in the vicinity of Verdun.

At the outbreak of the war Driant was enlisted as a reservist and posted at Verdun. He immediately took the step of requesting active service and, despite his age (he was over 60), was given command of two units. These were sent to the Bois des Caures, a key position in the first line of defences, on the right bank of the Meuse and to the north-east of Verdun. It did not take long for him to recognize that his forces were severely overstretched, and could not possibly man the position, let alone ensure that it was made immune to attack. He had neither the men nor the materials to bolster the ailing line.

In August 1915, after a period of some weeks during which his requests for reinforcements were simply ignored, Driant wrote to a personal friend who happened to be the President of the Chamber of Deputies. In the letter, he bemoaned the fact that he was unable to carry out adequately the tasks before him and outlined the reasons why. It is not clear whether Driant was attempting to use his political influence to change matters, or simply venting his frustrations. Either way, the letter was despatched to the Minister of Defence, Joseph Galliéni, who arranged for an Army Commission delegation of Deputies to be sent to the Verdun region in early December 1915.

Its inspection and subsequent report upheld Driant's original complaints. When Galliéni informed Joffre of the Commission's findings, the French Commander-in-Chief was uncharacteristically ruffled, and responded: 'I cannot be party to soldiers under my command bringing before the Government, by channels other than the hierarchic channel, complaints or protests concerning the execution of my orders'. He angrily concluded that, 'I consider nothing justifies the fear which, in the name of the Government, you express'. Such a riposte was coloured not only by the issue of hierarchy – which barely disguised Joffre's dislike of apparent political interference – but also his continuing insistence that the Germans presented no threat whatsoever to Verdun. Indeed, the Western Front as a whole, he believed, was 'unlikely' to see a German offensive in 1916. Instead, he held that they were more likely to make a push on the Eastern Front and in the direction of the Russian line. He felt, in consequence, that the 'commotion', as he saw it, being stirred by Driant and his political friends, was 'calculated to disturb profoundly the spirit of discipline in the Army'.

At the beginning of 1916, the *Grand Quartier Général* remained convinced that the Verdun sector was under no threat of serious or imminent attack. The *Stollen* were a defensive mechanism, proof that the Germans were digging themselves in; the deserters were simply over-reacting in their claims; aerial reconnaissance showed no signs of 'jumping-off' trenches being dug, a definite prerequisite to any major offensive move.

Why should anything other than a continued holding of the line be ordered?

The truth of the matter was that the Germans did not construct 'jumping-off' trenches because they believed they would not be required. An intense artillery barrage, of considerable duration, would mean that the attacking infantry could literally walk over much of the forward-lying French line. Resistance was not expected to be strong, where it existed at all. At least among those readying themselves for combat, the belief was that meticulous preparation was guaranteed to yield big advances early on.

A slight, yet perceptible, shift in French attitudes came about only in late January, as a consequence of the eventual, and belated, threading together of intelligence observations and other information and, possibly, a delayed reaction to the Army Commission's delegatory report. Eventually, alarm bells began to sound in the right quarters. On 24 January, Joffre's assistant, General de Castlenau, visited the Verdun zone and immediately ordered that all defensive works be switched to bulwarking the right-bank approaches to the city. As nerves began to strain further, Joffre himself made a visit to the front at Verdun. Thereafter, the race was on to build up Verdun's neglected defences as quickly and effectively as possible. Finally, on 12 February – the proposed day of the start of the German offensive – two divisions of reinforcements reached the RFV. Fortunately, as it turned out for the French, that day also brought with it snow blizzards that reduced visibility almost to zero. The onslaught would have to be postponed for 24 hours.

By February 1916 the Germans had assembled before Verdun a combined artillery and infantry force of massive proportions. This had been achieved at no small cost or effort. For an operation the size of the one planned, the sheer logistics involved in moving the required amount of men and munitions were quite staggering. One German historian has recently estimated the following: a single German infantry division of 16,000 men would have 7000 horses and 15 artillery batteries attached to it. Each of these batteries would require 36 ammunition trains which, in turn, would carry anything from 2000 heavy howitzer cannons to approximately 27,000 light artillery shells.

In terms of manpower, the Central Powers generally – and Germany in particular – found themselves overstretched by 1916 (though matters were to get considerably worse before the war ended). In 1914, no one had envisaged a lengthy campaign (the German Crown Prince had even alluded to a 'crisp, cheerful war') and so the matter of replacing those killed or disabled in combat had to be worked out on an *ad hoc* basis.

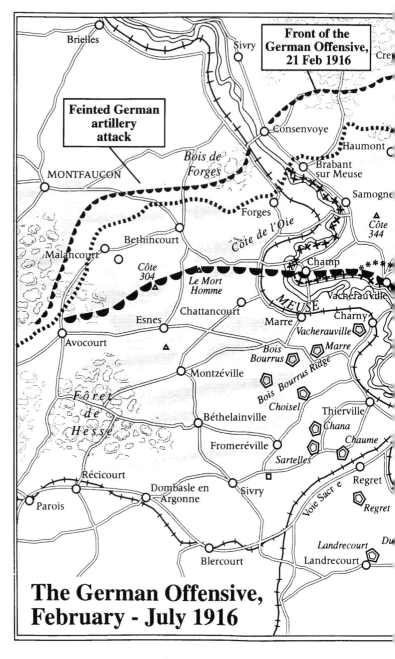

Brielles · Sivry · Cre

Front of the German Offensive, 21 Feb 1916

Feinted German artillery attack

Consenvoye

Haumont

Bois de Forges

Brabant sur Meuse

MONTFAUCON

Samogne

Forges

Côte de l'Oie

Côte 344

Béthincourt

Champ

Malancourt

Côte 304

Le Mort Homme

MEUSE

Vacherauville

Chattancourt

Marre

Charny

Esnes

Vacherauville

Avocourt

Bois Bourrus

Marre

Montzéville

Bois Bourrus Ridge

Forêt de Hesse

Choisel

Thierville

Béthelainville

Chana

Fromeréville

Chaume

Sartelles

Récicourt

Regret

Dombasle en Argonne

Sivry

Voie Sacré e

Parois

Regret

Landrecourt

Du

Blercourt

Landrecourt

The German Offensive, February - July 1916

2   The German Offensive on Verdun, February–July, 1916

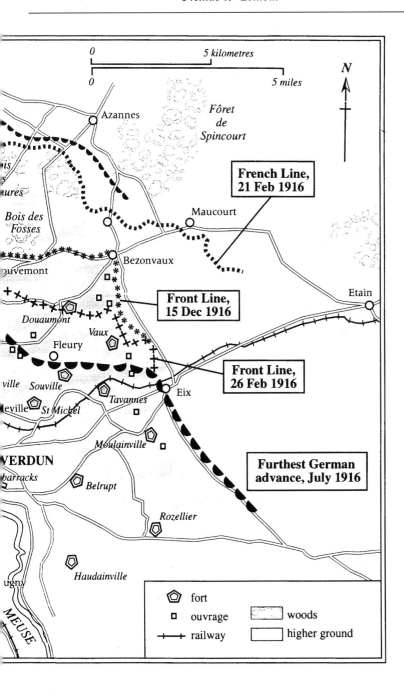

0   5 kilometres

0   5 miles

N

Azannes

Fôret de Spincourt

French Line, 21 Feb 1916

Maucourt

Bois des Fosses

Bezonvaux

ouvemont

Etain

Front Line, 15 Dec 1916

Douaumont

Vaux

Fleury

Front Line, 26 Feb 1916

ville   Souville

Tavannes   Eix

eville   St Michel

Moulainville

VERDUN

barracks

Belrupt

Furthest German advance, July 1916

Rozellier

Haudainville

ugny

MEUSE

fort

ouvrage   woods

railway   higher ground

Phot. A. Menzendorf, Berlin.   Unsere Feinde   580

French colonial troops

Before the Battle of Verdun, Germany was struggling in this respect, and the concentration required for the Lorraine region at this time hardly helped the wider situation. For the French, the situation was even more precarious for they had lost an estimated 600,000 men since the outbreak of hostilities. Increasingly, they were forced to plunder the young male populations of their empire. Consequently, at Verdun, Madagascans, Senegalese, Moroccans, Tunisians, and Algerians were to all see active service.

The German Fifth Army was the vanguard of the attacking force at Verdun. It was commanded by Wilhelm, the Crown Prince of the German empire. The eldest son of Kaiser Wilhelm II was born at Potsdam on 6 May 1882. As tradition dictated, he received an honorary military rank on reaching his tenth birthday, becoming a Lieutenant of the First

LITTLE WILLIE.

"WHO SAID VERDUN?"

'Little Willie': The Crown Prince, Wilhelm

Foot Guards. After graduating from university at Bonn, the Crown Prince travelled extensively throughout Asia. On returning to Germany, he became a cavalry regiment commander in 1911. Yet he took little active interest in learning the military profession and never received more than a basic training in it. Most of his time was spent either in a frivolous manner – he had a colourful private life that was the subject of much speculation – or by meddling in the affairs of state, especially matters of foreign policy. Both these traits annoyed many establishment figures in Germany, and they were further vexed by some of his more extreme views: he adhered closely to pan-Germanic ideals, for example, which he was never shy of articulating.

He had an oddly distant relationship with his father and one that often appeared strained. He had little or no significant influence over the Kaiser who, in turn, rarely sought advice from his son or held serious counsel with him. Nevertheless, and despite his almost amateur status, the Crown Prince was drafted in to take command of the Fifth Army in August 1914, replacing its injured commanding officer, General von Eichhorn. He immediately proved himself unable to follow orders and marched his men from Longwy-Longuyon – where he attacked the French – to the environs of Verdun, coming to a halt at the Meuse foothills. During the Battle of the Marne, the Fifth Army, by dint of its location, was drawn into the general retreat across the River Aisne. Thereafter, all became relatively quiet as Wilhelm observed the general defensive German position along the Western Front.

His first and only real opportunity for a moment of military glory was presented at the Battle of Verdun. If this confrontation was to be won by calibre of troops alone, his chances were better than average. The men of the Fifth, clad in their highly effective *feldgrau* combat fatigues and *stuhlhelm* helmets (which weighed nearly 6 kilograms), were a hardened bunch of fine soldiers who probably deserved an equally experienced commander. The army's ranks contained veterans of all the major Western Front campaigns to date – Ypres, the Marne – and had experienced the French offensives at Artois and Champagne.

The first German divisions placed at Verdun (forty-eight in total would see action there in 1916) were some of the best in the whole of the German Army. The attacking front line consisted of: the VII Reserve Corps, commanded by General von Zwehl; the XVIII Corps, under General von Schwenk; the III Corps – the famed Brandenburgers, considered to be one of the crack units of the army – under General von Lochow; and the V Reserve Corps, a little behind the first line, who were to be deployed in a holding position if need be until all assault troops had been fully mobilized. German reserves for the Verdun front comprised two divisions of the XV Corps. These were *in situ* in the Woërve region, south-east of Verdun, ready to advance as part of a general mopping-up process once the signal had been given that the French line had folded.

By February 1916 these men had been tempered for combat. The French historian, Georges Blond, has noted: 'The disposition of the German troops [at Verdun], with their supporting artillery and complex supply organisation, had been planned down to the last detail'. Morale was exceptionally high. The belief had filtered down to the rank-and-file from the Crown Prince's headquarters that victory was virtually assured. The infantry had seen the artillery amassed and, while this gave the men cause to ponder their own mortality, it also served to reassure and undeniably bolstered confidence. The feeling was prevalent that, once the

Pétain holds court at a French War Cabinet meeting

artillery had done its job, once the French line had been suitably 'soft-ened', the infantry could advance over the battered enemy line with 'guns slung from shoulder straps'. The novelty of pursuing an offensive strategy seemed to have come as a welcome diversion from the dreary day-to-day realities of life on the Western Front.

The French, by comparison, were in a state of some disarray and hope-lessly outnumbered. Following the relief of the Second Army by the British at the start of the year, their forces were focused around General Chrétien's XXX Corps. This included: the 72nd Division, commanded by General Bapst; the 51st Division, under General Boullangé; and the 14th Division, headed by General Crepey. In reserve was the 37th African Division of the Corps, commanded by General de Bonneval. All of this force was concentrated on the right bank of the Meuse. On the left bank was situated part of the VII Corps – the 29th and 67th Divisions – under General Bezelaire. Reserves were thin on the ground and some distance from Verdun, and comprised three divisions of the II Corps under General Duchesne. Further back still was the 48th Infantry Division. On its way up to Verdun was General Balfourier's XX Corps. This group proved to be the first relieving French force when it reached the battle zone on 23 February.

Like their German counterparts, the French forces, who had been hastily assembled in defence of Verdun in early 1916, were first-rate sol-diers and mostly hardened veterans of the Western Front and trench life, having seen action in all the major offensive and defensive actions of 1914 and 1915. Known as *poilus* – which alluded to facial hair, and which the

French infantry at Verdun

The *poilus*, backbone of the defence of Verdun

troops themselves largely resented for it was pointed out that if they *could* shave in a trench in a battle zone, then they *would* – they were renowned for their amazing *esprit de corps* and cutting sense of humour which derived as much from cynicism as from hardship. By 1916, French troops were fitted in a manner more suited to modern warfare. Gone were the impractical kepi head piece and conspicuous red tunics and bright-blue pantaloons of 1914. These had been replaced by steel 'Albert' helmets and a heavy *horizon bleu* uniform which, despite its usually rough cut, blended in well when muddied and so served adequately as camouflage.

Dictating the every move of these troops was a philosophy – set on high and implemented via a ruthless system of courts martial – of *L'attaque à outrance*, 'attack to excess'. This strategy invoked the belief that, in essence, offence was the principal and only viable form of defence, imprudence the best of assurances. If the enemy should gain any degree of initiative, or make a successful advance, every French soldier knew that he must attempt to win back these losses, regardless of costs and however unfavourable the odds. Conversely, every centimetre of ground – however untenable – was to be defended to the death. Obviously, such practice resulted, time and again, in needless slaughter. Surprisingly, however, there was no general questioning of this diktat, at least not until the later stages of the war. The *poilus* merely followed orders, most with a characteristically laconic shrug of the shoulders.

In terms of artillery pieces and weaponry, the French were simply outclassed by the Germans at Verdun in February 1916. As has been previously described, Verdun had been largely stripped of its heavy artillery simply because the upper echelons of the French Army had little belief in the effectiveness of such guns or other more modern inventions, such as the machine gun. It was a widely held, if somewhat romantic, notion that the strength of France's forces lay in its mobility so there was a heavy reliance on the quick-firing, light 75-mm field gun and bayonets (neither were much use on a static battlefield like the Western Front). As a result, in 1914 the whole of the French Army possessed only about 300 heavy artillery guns, and these were mostly outdated 120-mm pieces or 270-mm mortars built in the late nineteenth century.

The Germans, on the other hand, relied on heavy guns (150s, 210s) and super-heavy guns (280s, 305s) the last being capable of launching a shell weighing more than 700 pounds over a distance of some 10 kilometres. Furthermore, the Germans had a relatively new and ultra-powerful weapon available to unleash at Verdun, to which the French had no answer. The 420-mm. 'Big Bertha', developed by the armament manufacturers, Krupp, weighed over a ton. In previous outings its effects had been devastating, and had largely accounted for the Belgian forts in 1914.

Artillery

The heavy concentration of artillery pieces in the Meuse region before the assault on Verdun in 1916 ensured that, from the beginning, the battle was directed by the actions of heavy guns. Little altered in this respect throughout the ten-month duration of the conflict. In practical terms, it meant that the tactical advantage across the battlefield tended to be held by the force whose artillery was performing better. Effective counter-artillery work was always likely to pay the dividend of holding up the opposing infantry, however.

High-calibre guns and projectiles formed the backdrop against which all activities took place at Verdun in 1916. At the height of the conflict, not a moment passed when the screeching of falling shells could not be heard. And no one who served there could have done so without witnessing the gruesome consequences of explosives and shrapnel.

The 1200 artillery pieces assembled by the Germans for the February offensive gave them a superiority of four to one over France, partly reflecting the fact that the defence was generally ill-equipped in terms of heavier guns. Dependent on older, more cumbersome models, it would take the French considerable time and effort before they were able to match their adversaries – in terms of artillery – at Verdun.

Consequently, the French relied on lighter field pieces, such as the 75 mm, which could be set effectively to work at close and at longer range firing shells that weighed up to 16 Ib. The Germans had a similar weapon, the 77 mm. which was employed in conjunction with the 150-mm field howitzer.

But it was in the clinical use of heavier-calibre guns that the Germans excelled and which, in the formative phase of the battle, almost bought them a stunning victory at Verdun. Every calibre of gun had a designated task to perform. The 210 mm-Mörser, which could launch projectiles weighing up to 185 Ib, and 280 mm. howitzers, were both aimed at disrupting supplies of men and material up the French line; 305-mm Austrian mortars would be directed over the front line; and the super-heavy 420-mm 'Big Bertha' – firing ten rounds an hour of shells that weighed over 2000 Ib – was directed against fortifications and other fixed targets.

The French had nothing to compare with this brutal array of weaponry. In the early months of the battle, 120-mm pieces were used sporadically and against variable targets, leaving the much-fêted 270-mm mortar as the mainstay of the defensive battery. Commissioned in 1885, this weapon served the French well, and could launch a variety of shells over a distance of some kilometres. It was only in the later stages of the battle, following the collapse of the advance on Verdun, that heavier guns were introduced to the battle by the French as a means of augmenting the counter-offensive against the Germans. Some 400-mm naval guns were employed but their use was limited to longer ranges over which their impact was greatest. More notably, 370-mm pieces were unleashed to great effect. These were massive machines – the gun alone weighed nine tonnes – capable of firing shells that weighed in excess of 1000 Ib. It was in the aftermath of work by these guns that the French infantry was able to reclaim ground previously lost during German offensive operations.

Between them, the French and German armies expended over 10,000,000 shells at Verdun in one of the most indiscriminate and ferocious examples of artillery warfare ever seen. Across the narrow parcel of land to the north of the city, which served as the battlefield in 1916, the landscape was forever reshaped out of all recognition. The consequences of this are there to be seen even today.

A French artillery gun in action

The sheer scale of these guns meant that 'houses were dwarfed beside them and [they were] so heavy that it seemed the pavement might crumble'. But therein lay the rub. They were very difficult to move – especially in bad weather and across boggy battlefields – and took some sixty men and twenty-four horses to shift. They were also technically quite complex, and the effort of setting them up was considerable. Nevertheless, their presence had not only devastating practical consequences, but intense psychological ones, too. A French artilleryman, Henry Croisilles, remembered the German heavy guns at Verdun: '. . . vomit[ing] forth their fire: they resemble fierce gorgons, insatiable and intoxicated in

A German 210 mm. Mörser artillery piece

Shells stockpiled for use at Verdun

their fury. Detonations and explosions are blended together. The noise is like the wild gallopade of heavy monsters over vast, resounding metal plates.' Barrages such as this could – and regularly did – drive men insane.

By the eve of the onslaught, the Germans had assembled outside Verdun an amazing 1200 artillery pieces of varying calibre, and enough

1018. *LA GRANDE GUERRE* **1914-16** — *Bombardement de VERDUN - Ruines près du Canal*

Phot-Express - Visé Paris 1018

The consequences of long-range, heavy German artillery fire

ammunition for some hundreds of hours of barrage, concentrated to attack along a front stretching a little over 12 kilometres. Every weapon in this vast armoury had a designated purpose. The 420s, for example – of which there were thirteen at Verdun – were to be directed against the major forts; 305-mm mortars would be used against the French front lines; while the much feared and very effective 210s would range on the rear lines and aim to disrupt supplies and reinforcements to the front. For closer-range combat, the attackers had an array of weapons at their disposal, mostly lighter, rapid-firing guns (130s and 150s) which would operate under the umbrella of the heavier guns. They also had 77-mm field guns – comparable to the French 75s – and mine-throwers. For use in face-to-face combat, the Germans had a novel new product of their expansive war industry, the flame-thrower, which was unleashed on a mass scale for the first time at Verdun. This was a sinister cylindrical instrument that spurted boiling jets of liquid, causing, if not instant death, then severe burning. The only way to try to fight the immediate effects of this weapon, it seemed, was to roll on the ground and hope not to be hit by a shell or a bullet in the mean time.

Another new weapon to make an impression at Verdun was the use of air support for ground forces. In the course of the war, this particular strand of warfare had already attracted great popular appeal and made national heroes out of some pilots: Max Immelman of Germany and Georges Guynemer of France, for example. The aircraft used at Verdun were basic and sparsely equipped for combat. Battle tactics, too, tended to be rather elementary. As Horne points out, however, 'at Verdun, history was to be made in the air. For the first time aircraft were used en masse in support of ground tactics.'

In line with their extensive preparations on the ground, the Germans utilized the bulk of their air forces in the Verdun region for the battle, moving 168 planes, 14 balloons, and 4 Zeppelins to the area. These were meant to provide a 24-hour 'aerial barrage', designed to exclude French intelligence missions over the line and to protect the artillery positions. The tactic worked well for a time, mainly because the French were slow to employ any kind of air tactics or support (although in this department, they tended to suffer because the military had been reluctant to advocate the expansion of the air services at the start of the war when France had less than 150 fighting aircraft). The Germans, then, had the advantage in the air at the start of the offensive – their aircraft outnumbering the French five to one – and they were able to exploit their numerical superiority and the slight tactical edge that they had. With time, however, this situation was addressed and, in May, a unit of volunteer American fighters, the Lafayette Squadron, entered the fray on behalf of France. They were to make a significant contribution to the outcome of the battle in the air during the summer months.

But it was on the ground that the Battle of Verdun was to erupt one cold but clear February morning. Quite literally, France did not know what had hit it.

3

The Onslaught

When war begins Hell opens . . .

THE BATTLE OF Verdun was coloured, and in some vital respects controlled, by a number of key factors that lay beyond the control of all those involved. Firstly, the climatic extremes characteristic of that part of France – inclement and wet in winter with flooding, heavy mists, and fog; baking hot and dry throughout the summer – added greatly to the misery and suffering of the combatants on both sides. And once the effects of heavy shelling had ravaged the landscape, the weather increasingly impeded all military efforts on the ground. Secondly, the actual terrain upon which the battle was waged was to be of no small significance. The city of Verdun itself is the central convergence point of a natural geographic fortification formed by the hilly and complex rolling lands of the Meuse region. On the right bank of the River Meuse, to the north and east of the city, are steep ridges, easily defended but equally difficult to attack. Thick woodland carpeted much of this area until 1916 and provided excellent cover for artillery and infantry movement alike. It was mostly here, on a narrow front barely 20 square kilometres long, that the battle for Verdun was to be contested.

Blocking the German advance upon the city was a series of fortresses, varying in size and significance, which had been constructed in dense lines between 4 and 10 kilometres from the outskirts of the city. If the Germans were to succeed in either their primary aim of causing the French maximum losses for the least possible cost, or their secondary aim, of capturing Verdun, then these forts would either have to be overcome or effectively disabled. This would not be a straightforward task. The biggest of the forts were located atop the heights of the right-bank ridges to the north of Verdun, converging in a concentric manner, and therefore functioning as formidable defences ahead of the city.

The biggest fortress was at Douaumont. Because of its size (it dominated the surrounding countryside and its guns were positioned to sweep all that lay before it) and its location (it was the fortification closest to the German line), it was an integral feature of the entire battle zone and a key

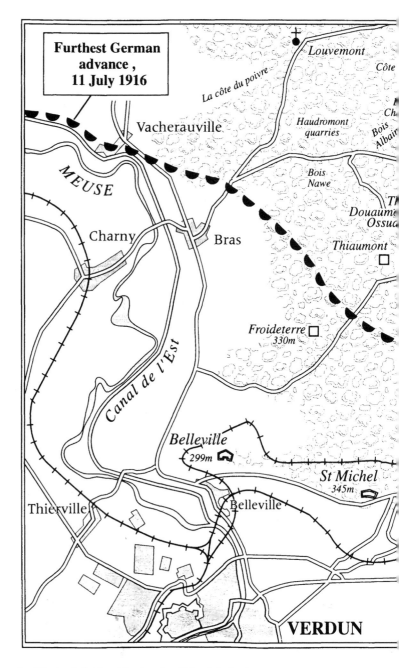

Furthest German
advance ,
11 July 1916

La côte du poivre

Louvemont

Côte

Ch

*Haudromont
quarries*

*Bois
Albai*

Vacherauville

MEUSE

*Bois
Nawe*

Tł
Douaumṭ
Ossua

Charny

Bras

Thiaumont

Froideterre
330m

Canal de l'Est

Belleville
299m

St Michel
345m

Thierville

Belleville

VERDUN

3   The battlefield and landmarks of the right bank

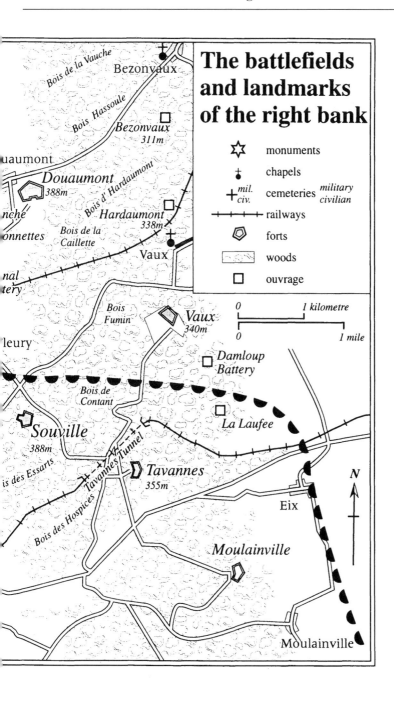

The battlefields and landmarks of the right bank

☆ monuments

† chapels

+ cemeteries military civilian

+++++++ railways

forts

woods

☐ ouvrage

0 ——— 1 kilometre

0 ——— 1 mile

Bois de la Vauche

Bezonvaux

Bois Hassoule

Bezonvaux
311m

uaumont

Douaumont
388m

Bois d' Hardaumont

nche

Hardaumont
338m

onnettes

Bois de la
Caillette

Vaux

nal
tery

Bois
Fumin

Vaux
340m

leury

Damloup
Battery

Bois de
Contant

La Laufee

Souville
388m

is des Essarts

Bois des Hospices

Tavannes Tunnel

Tavannes
355m

Eix

N

Moulainville

Moulainville

point, or obstacle, in the German line of attack. South-east of Douaumont was Fort Vaux, a smaller yet equally important fortress from a strategic point of view. These forts had come under heavy German artillery fire in February 1915 – one of the few instances of combative action along the Verdun front that year. They had, however, withstood the attack and their (yet to be dismantled) guns managed to repel an attempted enemy advance. Other smaller fortresses – at Souville, Belleville, St Michel, Tavannes, and Moulainville – lay between Vaux and the northern boundaries of the city. The land here featured a number of belatedly constructed trenches and hastily erected rows of barbed wire but, because their effectiveness was yet to be tested, their tenability remained open to question.

On the eve of the German attack, life in the city went on remarkably unaffected. There existed a general air of calm that might have suggested to the unknowing eye that little had changed from peacetime. This atmosphere endured in spite of a heightening of military activity in the area, with more troops and members of the General Staff, as well as extra artillery pieces, present in and around the city. But, for a garrison town, this was the norm and, to the unobservant or disinterested civilian, would have meant very little. It was true that the population of the city had been reduced by some four-fifths to a little over 3000 but the enlarged military presence served only to disguise this reduction of the civilian community. Moreover, for those civilians still present in Verdun at this time, life was good, especially for those in a position to benefit financially from troops desperate to enjoy precious time on leave.

Such relative tranquillity – and the appearance of life continuing more or less unaffected by the war – vanished in the space of a day. At a stroke, Verdun was transformed from one of the quietest towns along the Western Front into the epicentre of a mighty, man-made tempest.

The bad weather which descended upon the Verdun region on 12 February took some time to clear, and the poor visibility that this brought delayed the start of the German onslaught by some nine days. In the light of what was to unfurl at Verdun, this undoubtedly saved the French line from the catastrophe of oblivion. For, on 12 February, defensive preparations remained desperately inadequate. Crucially, the hiatus provided by the poor winter weather allowed this situation to be rectified to some extent.

As night fell on 11 February, the troops manning the French front lines were ordered to stand to, poised and ready for the attack that intelligence sources suggested was imminent. Fortunately, it did not materialize, allowing the reservists and engineers, who had been labouring for over two weeks, to continue the work of consolidating the first-

FRENCH INFANTRY AWAITING ORDERS AT VERDUN

French infantrymen awaiting orders at Verdun

and second-line defensive positions on the right bank while simultaneously completing the building of a vital intermediary line between the two. On the morning of 12 February, at the very moment the Germans had planned to rain shells upon the French part of the Verdun sector, this work was nowhere near completed. More time was required and, through the vicissitudes of the weather, this is exactly what the French got.

Over the next few days work continued unabated on these positions. Despite all the efforts of the French General Staff, however, the numbers of infantry and artillery pieces available for the defence of Verdun could not be bolstered. The French were short of heavy and light weapons alike, and barely had enough ammunition to service the guns they did have. And only thirty-four French battalions stood opposite seventy-four German battalions. In every respect then, the French forces could not match the Germans. This much was clear. The German artillery (including heavy guns) outnumbered that of the French by four to one, the ratio increasing to ten to one after the first round of heavy shelling. In the matter of infantry, the ratio at first favoured the Germans two to one, rising to three to one as the French sustained heavy losses within hours of the launching of the German artillery bombardment. With regard to the actual *materiel* of war, then, all that the extra time did for the French was to allow them time to consolidate those forces that were present in defence of Verdun. Other than this, the nine days served simply to lessen the element of surprise, if only slightly.

After a week of waiting, the weather finally broke on 19 February. That day, with the prospect of attack looming larger than ever, Joffre visited Verdun one last time before the German onslaught. After an inspection of the improved defensive works on the right bank, he paid hearty compliments to General Herr, even though these hasty, last-minute efforts, noble though they were, were far from sufficient. Undoubtedly, Joffre's praise must have rung hollow in the ears of Herr who had seen the wilful neglect of the RFV's defensive capacities proceed unabated over a period of some months.

The next day the sun shone brightly and the icy ground began to thaw. Everyone on the French side of the line immediately became more apprehensive because it was clear that, whatever might be in store for them, was now imminent. The mood along the line was mostly downcast. Driant wrote to his wife that he expected the front line where he was stationed to 'be taken in the first minutes' of any enemy attack. Further removed from the Verdun sector itself, confidence among the officers of the *Grand Quartier Général* was characteristically, if somewhat unjustifiably, high. In celebration of this confidence, or perhaps as a means of lifting flagging spirits and easing fraught nerves closer to the line, at 4 o'clock that afternoon the French artillery opened up for an hour-long bombardment of the German line. Later, Herr issued his final orders which contained the expected instruction to 'Resist whatever the cost'.

As night fell, the distant rumble of German munitions trains making their way towards the artillery positions was audible to the troops situated in the forward laying French line. Whether this noise conveyed to these men the sheer scale and extent of the attack that awaited them, no one really knows. Most would not survive to tell the story.

Across the zone still recognizable as no man's land, the German force stood primed to attack, awaiting the chance to unleash nine days' worth of nervous anxiety, brought on by the waiting game that seemed, to almost every soldier present, to have lasted an eternity. Every morning since 12 February, the infantry and the artillery had taken up their positions, only to be told to stand down for another twenty-four hours. This continual postponement led to widespread tension brought on by an exaggerated sense of expectation. The command of the Fifth Army became instantly aware that, with every passing day, the element of surprise upon which the success of their initial attack depended was lessened. Further, it was clear to see that the troops' general physical and psychological preparedness was waning with every passing hour. To address this problem, and as a means of keeping his soldiers' minds focused on the task in hand, on 12 February – hours after the first cancellation of the attack – the Crown Prince announced the following Order of the Day:

Let us realise to the full that the Fatherland expects great things of us. We must prove to the enemy that the iron will of the sons of Germany, set on victory, is still unbroken, and that the German army, when it advances to the attack, stops for no obstacle.

Yet such proclamations could barely quench fluttering nerves, nor could they reverse the fact that, as Wilhelm himself later observed, 'every hour lost meant a diminution of our prospects of speedy success'.

Nevertheless, with the turn in the weather, minds became clearly focused once more, and optimism rose perceptibly within all ranks of the German force assembled for the attack on Verdun. When the final order to take up positions was given, a wave of euphoria was released into the

A German trench at Verdun

air, and all the pent-up energies and anxieties which had been suppressed for over a week were discharged. Finally, the infantry would be free from the bleak, damp surrounds of their temporary accommodation, the stuffy underground *Stollen*, that had proven to be claustrophobic and suitable only for short-term living. There would be no more pointless drills, no more running through the same old routines that many felt made a mockery of all the hours and days of precise preplanning and training. Even more relieved, perhaps, were the gunners who would finally have the chance to aim at the French lines. They had been living for too long with the full implications of what was about to befall the enemy, and no person with any semblance of a conscience could have lived at ease with such knowledge. They simply wanted to get started, to be able to stop pondering the whys and hows of the attack.

On the eve of the offensive, the men assembled in barracks and canteens, ate and drank together, and wished one another luck. They took comfort from safety in numbers – quite literally – and in the widespread belief that ultimate victory was a mere formality. As military bands played sentimental farewell tunes, nervously composed messages were despatched to loved ones far away.

The artillery bombardment, the process of 'softening' the French line, which was to precede the advance of the assault troops, began at 07.15 hours in the emerging dawn of 21 February 1916. The sky was crystal clear, providing almost perfect conditions under which to launch an assault. Overnight, however, the ground under foot had once again frozen over, and this would make the job for the advancing infantry more difficult later on that day.

It would be nearly nine long hours before this unprecedented storm of steel lifted. Despite the continuing efforts of some of his closest advisers, and others in the command of the Fifth Army including the Crown Prince himself, Falkenhayn resolutely stuck to his initial plan of concentrating all offensive efforts along the right-bank approaches to Verdun, thereby circumscribing the density of the attack to the narrowest possible front. The precarious, exposed heights of the left bank would be attacked only if circumstances dictated that such an action was absolutely necessary.

From the start, the German artillery acted with the greatest precision and in the most direct manner. Rapid-firing 150-mm. and 130-mm field guns went to work on their designated task of reducing to rubble those French positions closest to the German line. Meanwhile, higher-calibre pieces – the 210 mm guns and 305 mm mortars – concentrated on hitting the area beyond the French front line, rendering useless any efforts that aimed to bolster the ailing defences with either men or materials.

The *Collége Buvignier*, Verdun, in the aftermath of a German artillery assault

Between early morning and the late afternoon of that first day of combat, the sky above the German line was coloured by a rainbow of flames, as an estimated 1,000,000 shells were fired, one quickly after the other. This was nothing other than an absolute demonstration of brute force on an industrial scale. There was no precedent, in this or any other war, for such a show. So enormous was the attack that its reverberations were immediately felt across a vast area of land. A French general, posted more than 100 miles away from the actual point of the offensive, recorded hearing clearly on the morning of 21 February, 'an incessant rumble of drums, punctuated by the pounding of big basses'. That such a din was audible so far away from the scene of the attack serves to illustrate the immense scale of the forces unleashed by the Germans at Verdun.

Uncharacteristically, perhaps, bearing in mind the overall accuracy and efficiency with which the German artillery performed that fateful morning, one of the first shells to be fired, from a 210-mm gun, landed some 30 kilometres away from its intended target – a bridge crossing the River Meuse – exploding in the courtyard of the Bishop's Palace at Verdun and destroying a part of the nearby cathedral. Nevertheless, this proved that the artillery had the capacity and the range for disrupting

French operations far beyond the front line. Later on in the day, the main railway station at Verdun was also shelled.

Further forward, the lighter field guns were devastating the French line. The right-bank defences were subjected to constant heavy shelling, with the soldiers positioned there being exposed to an incessant and deafening din as well as unimaginable dangers. The shock to each man caught in this unrelenting inferno was instantaneous and, once it set in, was never completely shaken off. One young artilleryman wrote of his experiences of that morning: 'Gradually the shells fall nearer [our position], a hundred yards away, then fifty, to [the] right and left of us, while shrapnel burst over our heads . . . [Later] there was a regular hailstorm of shells.'

Others noted how 'the human presence was reduced to flattened terror' by the shelling, as everywhere the earth erupted and shattered, entire areas of forest were uprooted, men's bodies ripped into bloody pieces, horses slaughtered on the spot. Nothing was safe from the effects of a bombardment that was readily penetrating the entire French position, from the front line to back beyond the city of Verdun itself. The French artillery could not find sufficient breaks in the attack to begin an effective rearguard action. Simultaneously, on the ground, most of the French-held positions were taken unawares. Within the first hour of the attack, French strongholds the length and breadth of the battle zone had been reduced to nothing. Communications channels between the front-line area and command posts were severed almost everywhere, and volunteer recruits were called upon to act as runners. Under such concentrated shelling, however, they neither got very far nor lasted for long. Consequently, entire divisions were left stranded, literally cut off from their command posts. Such circumstances meant that no one was quite sure how to react to the catastrophe that was unfolding around them. It would take some considerable time before confusion gave way to a degree of calm, and the prevailing situation of sheer panic began to subside.

Among the explosive shells was a smattering of gas-filled devices. Not for the first, nor the last, time in World War I, toxic warfare was unleashed with chilling consequences and in blatant disregard for resolutions drawn up at one of the earliest Hague Conventions. But the general state of play in the early morning of 21 February was such that this represented only one in a plethora of problems that faced the French. There was little that they could do to rectify this or any other matter.

The exposed infantry could do no more than hope to avoid falling explosives while, at the same time, hold their positions. It was imperative, moreover, that their cover held out. Where it did not – and many trenches and bunkers were levelled in an instant – they had to discover and take alternative shelter as quickly as was possible. Meanwhile, the commanding hierarchy to the rear – cut off as they were from developments in and around the battle zone – had to await the arrival of reliable information before they could make informed calculations and decisions, based on the general overall situation as they saw it. All this time, the artillery remained largely helpless, and was unable to launch any kind of meaningful counterstrokes because, with smoke filling the air and clouding all vision, observation was severely restricted. Furthermore, many cannons were obliterated, blown to bits, before there was any chance to utilize them. Over the course of the day, the only successes enjoyed by the French proved to be incidental and at the longest of ranges.

Throughout the initial phases of the attack, the weather remained remarkably bright for the time of year. Consequently, the German air force was able to work effectively in conjunction with ground forces and in its own right. Not only did it have a clean sweep of the skies above Verdun but, owing to the sheer speed of the attack, French aircraft remained grounded all day. Artillery planes were able repeatedly to target and hit a number of key locations across the battle zone. Meanwhile, observation craft, untroubled by the enemy, enjoyed complete freedom and the only restriction they experienced was from the obscurity caused by the after-effects of the general bombardment.

At about midday, the onslaught was brought to a temporary halt. In this way, the German commanding staff hoped that the shaken French infantry would be persuaded to reveal themselves – if only momentarily – and, at the same time, expose those sections of the front-line trenches that had so far withstood the best efforts of the first waves of shelling. Many were too canny to fall into such a trap, others too scared. But, in one or two places, the plan did yield dividends.

The 210-mm guns, meanwhile, returned to the task of attacking the area furthest from the front. The efficacy of these heavier guns was such that the French ability to bring up reinforcements was severely limited. The back-up forces that did manage to reach forward positions merely suffered the same terrible and unsustainable losses as the infantry already in place, often without managing to find cover. That first day many died without ever seeing the enemy, a circumstance that was to characterize the entire Battle of Verdun.

Across the whole war zone, French forces were really being bled to death. Serious damage was being inflicted yet no adequate response could be mustered. In a communiqué to the rear – which may have got through at the intended time – one French corporal reported that, by the early afternoon of 21 February, out of every five men under his command, 'two have been buried alive under their shelter, two are wounded to some extent or other, and the fifth is waiting . . .'. Whichever way one viewed it – and the French General Staff were prone initially to take the most favourable view they could – the general situation was extremely bleak. Meanwhile, the German infantry simply waited for the 'softening' to come to an end and for the signal to advance to be passed down the line.

The German artillery continued to work as one, with monstrous consequences. The attackers were wiping out all that lay before them. The initial stage of Falkenhayn's scheme was unfurling more or less as he had intended. In an order handed down to the Fifth Army's command in early February, the German High Command had underlined the necessity to impress on 'both infantry and artillery' the need 'to prevent the attack being brought to a standstill at any point, and thus afford the French no respite'. Certainly, on 21 February, this injunction was carried out to the letter. The force of the artillery was levelling and reshaping the whole environment of the battlefield in its own gruesome fashion. Men were being pulverized into a gory mess of burning flesh and blood, disappearing into the earth only to be disinterred by the next shell falling. Typically, a shell might account for fifteen men dead and another ten wounded; sometimes the casualty figures were lower than this, often they were much higher.

As entire units were hammered into the ground where they stood, the turmoil that had engulfed the French lines worsened by the minute. Worst of all for the men on the ground, any cover that existed was liable to be blown away. Georges Blond has retold how, 'Trenches of normal depth in the course of a few minutes were opened up as if by a giant hand, and turned into deep pits lined with corpses and fragments of corpses'. In the trenches around the Bois des Herbebois, on the French line closest to the German position, it was estimated that, on the first day of the assault on Verdun, a French soldier was mortally wounded on average once every five minutes. Here, as elsewhere in the battle zone, French forces were – after little more than an hour or so of the bombardment – reduced to fending for themselves in the open, because any defensive cover had been completely destroyed or rendered hazardous by the enemy's artillery fire.

Death added an almost surreal atmosphere to the day's proceedings. Yet, in the midst of such bedlam, no one had much of a chance to take in the general scene let alone comprehend the grave losses being inflicted at close quarters. The countryside was soon completely peppered with shell craters that could measure anything up to 12 metres in diameter. As this lunar landscape was created, anything in the path of an exploding shell – man, animal, or plant life – was likely to be annihilated and then hurled high into the air. Debris of every variety and shape lay scattered everywhere across the battlefield. The defending line was in as much danger from the secondary fall-out created by the bombardment as from the primary explosions. One French soldier observed 'a tree-trunk from a gun emplacement sail over my head as gracefully as if it had been a tennis ball'. But such extraordinary experiences paled when compared to the crackling sound of exploding shells, the booming of distant guns, the shaking ground underfoot, the blazing crimson-fire winter sky above, and the shrieking of wounded men crying out in agony for aid that could not be given under the torrent of enemy shells. Another infantryman was later to recall his experiences in the French line that day:

> For an eternity we listen to the iron sledgehammers beating upon our trench . . . Amid this tempest of ruin we instantly recognise the shell that is coming to bury us. As soon as we pick out its mournful howl we look at each other in agony. All curled and shrivelled up, we crouch under the very weight of its breath. Our helmets clang together, we stagger about like drunks.

Despite their early morning optimism and high expectations, as the day wore on matters worsened for the awaiting German infantry. Soon, their only comfort was that it was *their* artillery positions that were hammering away, the enemy who were managing only a fitful and ineffectual response. They stood motionless and shivering in muddy trenches, trying as best they could to block out the tempest that was raging overhead. But such a feat was near impossible to perform. Nerves were heightened by the apparent impunity of the heavy guns – after all, this might one day soon happen to them – and the knowledge that, shortly, they would be called upon to execute the next stage of Operation *Gericht*.

It was only as a result of fading daylight that the barrage of artillery fire began to ease. The German infantry would have its part to play in the action before nightfall. Meanwhile in the approaching twilight, across a no man's land barely discernible through the clouds of smoke and dust, French survivors had perhaps their first chance to take full stock of the horrors that had befallen them. Many men had been physically maimed that day at Verdun; all had been mentally affected to some degree. The realization that all sense of humanity, of common reason, had been dispersed in an instant, began to take a hold. But such feelings, palpable though they were, could not be easily articulated, such was the incomprehensibility of the situation.

Those not blinded by the smoke were choking on it. Gas victims strained for a last gasp of breath before expiring. The dead lay scattered everywhere, the injured lying among them barely distinguishable from the corpses. Limbs and hunks of flesh hung from tree stumps or were

ground into the muddy surface of the earth. Men still on their feet struggled to keep a footing on a surface of bloody, slimy pulp the consistency of
butter.

As snow started to fall the temperature dropped considerably, another
enemy against which the prostrate wounded had to battle. Still no
stretcher-bearers could attend to the fallen. Such unfortunates either gave
in completely or clung on for dear life, hoping against hope that the
enemy barrage would soon come to an end, allowing first-aiders to enter
the battle zone. Some were happy simply still to be alive though those in
excruciating pain might have pleaded with a nearby comrade to end their
misery with a merciful bullet. Others knew that the end was close at hand
and resigned themselves.

Away from the front line, the French response remained largely insignificant. Where its positions were not completely cut off either by a dense
screen of smoke or a lack of communication, the artillery found it difficult
to muster any kind of a response. The Germans had accurately pin-
pointed a number of batteries and rendered them inactive. Therefore,
when orders were received later in the day, the riposte was, at best, feeble,
at worst, non-existent. Reinforcing infantry units similarly found positive
action difficult. They struggled to relieve isolated pockets of soldiers on
the field of action as they invariably could not weave their way through
the bombardment. The command, meanwhile, had no realistic idea as to
what was unravelling ahead of the city of Verdun. Only limited intelligence, of questionable validity, was reaching them. As a result, it was
difficult to piece together an accurate picture of what was occurring. At 3
o'clock that first afternoon, an official communiqué was released that
barely alluded to the terrors of the previous eight hours: 'Slight activity on
both sides along the whole front, except to the north of Verdun, where
fire developed considerable intensity'. This was the first that the French
nation was to hear of the Battle of Verdun.

The command of the Fifth Army could barely contain its pleasure at the
apparent ease with which its artillery was operating. Scenes of near ecstasy
greeted the earliest intelligence reports from the front. From vantage
points, the Crown Prince was able to survey the damages that his forces
were managing to inflict upon the enemy. A decisive victory looked like
being no more than a formality and morale was boosted accordingly.

Shortly before 4 o'clock that first afternoon, the order was sent down
the line to the awaiting infantry. They would proceed to advance on the
hour. The sense of release in the trenches was tangible. These assault
troops – fully prepared and equipped with detailed maps and sufficient
supplies – would be accompanied 'over the top' by squadrons of

machine-gunners whose job would be to help weed out any pockets of resistance.

The advance would not be one of linear formation but rather consist of a series of small, tightly formed units of men. It was calculated that, in this way, the forward-lying ground could be covered with the greatest efficiency and in utmost safety. Through wisps of smoke and over difficult terrain, the procession advanced at a slow walking pace. As predicted, guns hung heavily from shoulder straps at every man's side.

The aim of the infantry on that first afternoon was a predetermined one. The force was simply to probe the French line and 'feel out' the points where the bombardment had been most effective. In this respect, the first German infantry movements were about intelligence gathering and, theoretically at least, had little to do with conquest. Obviously, patrol leaders could occupy ground, but only when circumstances allowed this to be done in safety and with impunity. There was no general order to fill in seemingly devastated areas of the French line which might contain snipers, or where concealed points of resistance might linger. Casualties were to be kept to a minimum. A concentrated attacking movement was planned for the next day: this aimed to fill with infantry the holes created by the artillery.

The advance was an easy one and, for the most part, remained straightforward. At certain points along the front, assault troops passed over what had previously been French strongholds without even realizing they had done so. There remained in such places no obvious signs of what at dawn had been trenches, nor any other tell-tale indicators of the vanquished line such as sand-bagging or abandoned equipment. Human remains became evident only on closer inspection of the mangled earth.

It was apparent that, in some places, much of the French front line had been comprehensively destroyed. From across the narrow battle area, patrol leaders began urging their superiors that these massive successes should be exploited immediately and the attack scheduled for the next day brought forward. But night had fallen by the time these requests reached Falkenhayn and, cautious as ever, he resolutely refused to countenance any such moves under the cover of darkness. Yet, in practice and out in the battle zone, not everyone was to behave with the restraint expected and required of them. General von Zwehl's VII Reserve Corps, for example, was advancing in a line due north of the city of Verdun. Overcome by the thrill of the advance, which so far had entailed little of the hard work that might have been expected, caution was thrown to the wind and a deliberate deviation from the predetermined blue-print enacted. It was to bring the Germans their first concrete gains of the battle.

A German flame-thrower in action. This novel weapon was used on a mass-scale for the first time at the Battle of Verdun

Moving now in a slight south-westerly direction, Zwehl guided his men on to the approaches of the strategically important Bois d'Haumont. Once within the boundaries of what was left of the wood, the advancing force stumbled across the remnants of two exhausted defensive units. With large gaps evident along this overstretched line – the two units were holding perhaps a kilometre of the front between them – the French were easily overcome by rifle fire and flame-throwers. Thereafter, the advancing force eased through those parts of the line that had earlier been razed by the artillery. Within a short time, all remains of the trenches had been occupied by the attackers, and any other defensive positions overcome. The wood, which had been flattened by an estimated 80,000 shells raining down on an area of 900 by 450 metres, was then taken with relative ease and minimal effort. The Bois d'Haumont was the German forces' first, critical footing in the original French line.

Elsewhere on the field, as advances penetrated deeper, defensive resistance proved to be far more determined than at the Bois d'Haumont. Gradually, the pace of the forward march was slowed. Desperate though the situation facing most French survivors was, their hastily enacted rearguards followed to the letter the edict of dying on the spot rather than giving way to the enemy's advance. When they could fire, even some of the injured and prostrated did so. At an early and vital time, then, resistance began to stiffen and some sense of spirit was immediately restored to the battered ranks of the French infantry.

There were many instances of groups or individuals holding their nerve against all odds in the face of the gravest of dangers. At the Bois des Caures, a young lieutenant led a snap bayonet charge that saw the retaking of lost positions; at the same location, a sergeant had single handedly held up the German advance by launching a frenzied volley of hand-grenades. Under the circumstances, the strength of the advancing forces mostly proved to be irresistible and the already heavy French losses were greatly compounded. Recognizable, though moderate, damages were, for the first time at Verdun, inflicted upon the attacking forces, however. When opposing lines narrowed to the point where rifles became useless, bayonets, rifle butts, spades, rocks, and anything else that came to hand, were employed instead. Though in most cases short lived, fighting was intense demonstrating that, at this early stage, compassion was in short supply. The heavy toll in human life was escalating everywhere. Where resistance endured, speedily established machine-gun emplacements ensured that it was just as quickly crushed.

After a few eagerly contested hours, during which the fortitude of the French and the formidableness of the Germans were both illustrated, the fighting came to a temporary end. Night fell over Verdun. But there was to be no real or sustained respite.

The combined German forces' effort that first day had had an immeasurably large impact on the environment to the north of Verdun and on the French forces located there. The artillery barrage had been especially felt. One historian has described the area blitzed on 21 February as being:

> like the calcified surface of the moon or some other dead planet, with smoke hanging overhead. The desolate ground was covered with long necklaces, whose beads were bomb craters, outlining the former French trenches. Where there had been woods, all the branches had been lopped off, leaving an assembly of charred, bare trunks, a sort of tree cemetery, blanketed in snow.

The human effects were no less calamitous. An as yet incalculable number of men had been lost, wounded or dead, on the French side. Those who survived were deeply traumatized, suffering from mental and physical wounds that would not easily heal. One artilleryman admitted, 'that day was an inferno for all of us, and indeed I never expected to come out of it alive'.

During the evening, snow shrouded the German assault patrols that were to be found easing their way cautiously around the dark approaches of what constituted a new, ill-defined dividing line between the opposing forces. It was not long before the artillery once again started up the bombardment in the most furious manner. There was no significant let-up.

On the French side, they attended to their broken men and their broken defences, patching up both as best they could. But resources, which had been scant to begin with, were now stretched to the limit. Everything, it seemed, was in short supply. Nonetheless, a certain resolve in the face of adversity appears to have taken hold of the shell-shocked defensive line. In many instances – some too horrific to contemplate – the French had been completely crushed, pounded as they were by the incessant artillery fire, ravaged by ruthless assault patrols, and everywhere hampered by the human carnage and material debris that was to be found across the afflicted area. In spite of this, the line had held up remarkably well. There had been no capitulation, no rolling back in the direction of Verdun. Furthermore, resistance had been robust. There were cases where beleaguered units had been overwhelmed, allowing natural instincts to take control. Men had fled for cover, pulling back to a suitable shelter. But nowhere had the general order to 'resist whatever the cost' been wilfully disobeyed. Moreover, when the command to retake lost ground was given – and, in most cases, it was done instantly – not one man flinched from the task. With discipline maintained, there were scraps of encouragement for the French commanding generals. But these were all there was.

Conversely, the exhilaration felt earlier by many within the upper echelons of the German Fifth Army had, by evening, somewhat abated. The planned rapid advance had simply not materialized. This could be attributed to a number of factors but, primarily, French resistance had been far stronger than anyone had thought possible. In turn, this suggested that the artillery effort had proved to be less effective than expected.

It was also undeniable that, even at this early stage, tactical blunders had been committed. The initial advantage, the huge element of surprise, that the Germans had created with the force of their artillery barrage, had not been fully exploited. Ascendancy on the ground was established but not forcibly acted upon. Rather than allowing the assault troops the benefit of pushing on, Falkenhayn's caution dictated that, instead, they adhere precisely to his plans. Thus, by nightfall, German advances in some places could be measured in terms of metres rather than kilometres. The fact was instantly recognized, the frustration of it keenly felt.

One historian has suggested that, 'when it came to following up, the Germans appeared to lose faith'. The point is debatable. Certainly, the stringent German blue-print for that first day did not allow commanders on the spot enough leverage to make informed decisions upon which they could act. Falkenhayn's caution carried the day. His approach, however, was entirely consistent with his primary aim of drawing French forces out into a costly war of attrition (if not with the Crown Prince's designs on the fortress of Verdun). If this is actually what directed Falkenhayn's actions on 21 February – and it appears to be the most plausible explanation for what happened – then it would suggest that he was merely keeping faith with his original proposition and not allowing the momentum of events to overtake him.

Nevertheless, the inability to make further inroads into the French line was more than a little puzzling, especially given the huge efforts expended in front of Verdun that day. One French officer thought it 'a pitiful result to show for such an enormous expenditure of material resources and human effort'. But this reality hardly diminished the all too brutal consequences of what had happened. Moreover, there were more immediately pressing concerns for the French forces, namely, what the Germans would do next. No one could be totally sure. More of the same was expected but, with weather conditions worsening, uncertainty dictated that nobody could confidently predict exactly when, let alone how, this would occur. A French General, Cherfils, felt sure that the Germans – 'cautious and methodical' – were acting in a most calculated manner and would wait for the heavy artillery guns to roll into action again. Thereafter, he forecast, they would 'make sure of their foothold before taking another step'.

There was widespread unease among French officers that the attack would be broadened to encompass the left-bank approaches to Verdun thereby stretching scant resources ever further and taking the onslaught to an area where preparations were highly inadequate. While reducing the intensity of the offensive, however, such a move might actually have increased its overall effectiveness. Falkenhayn's insistence on restricting the initial attack to the narrowest of fronts was of enormous consequence, yet might have indirectly aided the French defence. Basil Liddell Hart observed that 'the few scattered packets of surviving Frenchmen [on 21 February] caused more delay than would have been possible on a frontage of rational width'. But, in the heat of the moment, this fact was less than readily apparent. Falkenhayn remained unflinching, assured in the knowledge that the French at Verdun were in disarray and that the initiative lay almost wholly with his forces.

There was to be no mercy shown. The offensive would remain inexorable. The morning of 22 February, it was determined, would be the time when the Germans would begin to avenge their 'poor' showing of the previous day. The initial plan of action for that second day of the Battle of Verdun was a near carbon copy of the first: the artillery would persist in 'softening' the French line in the morning; the infantry would follow up in the afternoon. The difference now was that there was to be no general restrictions placed upon the infantry advances by the High Command. In line with the predetermined timetable for Operation *Gericht*, assault troops would be ordered to fill the vacuums created by the artillery barrage and press the French line as far as possible.

Their opponents, however, were equally determined not to be caught out again to the same disastrous extent. The French were in defiant mood, resilient despite it all, prepared if necessary to play David to Germany's Goliath. They, too, were set on improving on their poor performance in the battle to date. Consequently, all infantry, exhausted though they were, were ordered to fulfil French military doctrine and hastily reclaim all lost ground. In a crucial respect, the French command was attempting to win back some of the initiative already forfeited to the Germans.

At this point, however, theory was easier espoused than put into practice. Nowhere could the French infantry hope to sustain adequately even the smallest advantage over the enemy. As best they could but in a necessarily restricted manner, they struck out at German assault units all along the contested front. Yet ultimately, a lack of strength in depth – in terms of weaponry and numbers – began to tell as did inadequate preparations and intelligence gathering. All morning the French were thwarted. The Germans had dug in well and established effective machine-gun posts. Consequently, they were well positioned to counter all French offensive moves and to hold the ground before another advancing movement. Meanwhile, the artillery bombardment continued uninterrupted.

Eventually, the French artillery managed to start firing and this gave a boost to the beleaguered front line. But the exhilaration, such as it was, was short lived. Most batteries were working well below par and in an ineffective manner. Worst of all, targets had either not yet been properly designated nor guns realigned following the effects of the earlier German bombardment. As a result, shells were being fired off-target, dropping short of the mark and in the vicinity of, or even *on to*, French positions. In

L'Actualité par la Carte Postale (1916)
Visé Paris 881
DES CANONS !..
DES MUNITIONS !..

A French propagandist's view of the artillery response at Verdun

this way, unnecessary casualties were added to the already high cost in human life.

Further self-inflicted wounds undermined French counter-moves all that day. An attempt to retake the Bois d'Haumont lapsed into farce because of last-minute hierarchical interference and because an under-strength force of poor calibre was entrusted to perform this most deadly of tasks. Isolated and working off his own initiative, a Lieutenant-Colonel Bonviolle spent the first night of the battle piecing together a planned pre-dawn counterstroke against the wood. But the arrival of a delayed runner – who had taken most of the night to reach his intended destination – with orders for a similar attack but at a later hour was followed by a conversation between Bonviolle and General Bapst, over a shakily restored telephone line, when Bapst ordered that the offensive be launched only after reinforcements had arrived. In consequence, the entire operation was subject to alteration and not launched until 08.30 hours in broad daylight but without the arrival of adequate reinforcements.

To hinder matters further, the Germans, who half expected such an assault, were able to second guess the plan when an intelligence aircraft spotted the French assembling before the wood. This force of mainly ageing reservists was no match for von Zwehl's doughty VII Reserve Corps. Under a hail of machine-gun fire, the French line was forced to fall back in a southerly direction to the village of Haumont which itself was under threat from another advancing German line. Hundreds of prisoners were taken (including officers) and a gaping chasm opened in the defensive line. In this instance, the pursual of *L'attaque à outrance* had back-fired with horrendous consequences.

From the French point of view, the situation was an ever-worsening one, and there was no time to consolidate, let alone improve matters. Troops everywhere were exposed and fighting unsupported. Yet the brutal pattern, which had emerged on the first afternoon, of French soldiers falling on the spot with a dogged determination rather than yielding to the enemy, was repeated across the battlefield. Retreat remained the last resort and for most was never even a feasible option.

The hole that had opened up ahead of the Bois d'Haumont was an obvious point of great vulnerability which the Germans immediately attacked. Around Haumont village their progress was temporarily arrested by some nimble machine-gunners. Further resistance was gallant, the fighting competitive. But, once the Germans introduced flame-throwers, the ultimate outcome was a foregone conclusion. Haumont village fell, with the French clinging on to the last and under the most intolerably unfavourable of circumstances.

The French command was now resolved that, if the oncoming enemy waves could not be repelled, they could at least be stemmed, hence buying valuable time for the rearguard. But such tactics cost dearly. After the fall of the position at Haumont, a mere sixty-four men remained alive out of a starting force estimated to have comprised eight companies. Moreover, logistics dictated that any hold-ups caused by the French at a given point on the front could not simultaneously be reproduced along the rest of the line. The block could not be made absolute. Therefore, holding actions of this nature and at such an early stage were largely futile exercises, and saw the loss of yet more human lives.

After Haumont, the Germans immediately switched their attention to the Bois des Caures which lay exposed to the east in a line almost parallel to Haumont. From a German viewpoint, the strategic significance of this wood could not be underestimated because its flanking positions rendered vulnerable those gains already made. In their determination to take it, they would assemble the best part of three corps' worth of assault troops.

The infantry attack was preceded with the usual heavy artillery barrage, merciless in its intensity. The already pulverized forest was in places completely cleared by the bombardment. Remaining trenches, along with other defensive footholds, were levelled and communications channels were rendered impotent. Thus, the defensive force was cut off and engulfed on all sides by the enemy.

As an important front-line position, the Bois des Caures had been relatively well manned before 21 February. By the time the Germans

The scene at the Bois des Caures on 22 February 1916, following a brutal German assault. It was in defence of this position that Lt.-Col. Emile Driant fell, thus becoming France's first national hero of the Battle of Verdun

advanced upon it for a direct attack, however, Lieutenant-Colonel Driant's forces had been reduced to just two understrength battalions. It was yet another hopeless situation, characterized by the now-expected defensive defiance. Driant himself was to fall in defence of the wood, preventing the ignominy of a certain court martial for his earlier perceived insubordination before Joffre, and bringing him the status of France's first hero of the Battle of Verdun.

In this instance, the casualties inflicted were some of the heaviest France had yet suffered. Troops were forced to fight in the open after 'our shelters began to disappear under the shower of 210 and 305 mm shells, not to mention trench-mortar bombs of all sizes'. As the bombardment lifted, the German infantry attacked through the open gaps which had been carved in the French position. The exposed defenders now became easy prey to the advancing forces, dazed as they were by the numbing experience of the artillery fire which had seen an estimated 10,000 tons of shells dropped on the wood already. There were few survivors: less than 100 from an estimated 1200 Frenchmen who began the day in the wood.

General von Lochow's Brandenburgers, meanwhile, were attacking to the north of the Bois des Caures in support of the action there. But their advance was slowed by a desperate French rearguard action. A frantic volley of machine-gun fire not only prevented an immediate German advance, it also inflicted notable losses, the highest single incidence of German casualties to date. This had the effect of partly deflating the high confidence within the ranks of the III Corps.

Nonetheless, what had been wrought upon the German line here was no more than an aberration, a minor set-back as they saw it. Everywhere else along the front the French were being relentlessly pushed back and slaughtered despite all resistance. By the end of the day, the combined successes of the German infantry were such that all the French first line had been conquered save for the villages of Brabant and Herbebois. It was only a matter of time before these fell, too, and such was their vulnerability that the French command even discussed their abandonment. All the time, the loss of human life could not be stemmed. France continued to bleed, though the Germans were now suffering the odd abrasion.

French commanders were everywhere beset by confusion. They were now expected to restore order out of the prevalent chaos by making hasty decisions under the most wretched of conditions. It was a near impossible job, as illustrated by the case of General Bapst. The elderly general knew only too well that French Army doctrine dictated that all ground must be held however untenable it might seem to be and regardless of cost. But surveying the overall situation, he was also aware that resources were stretched to the limit. Overwhelming logic prescribed that, following the losses of Haumont and the Bois des Caures, remaining divisions in the north of the battle area – who were desperately needed to defend more southerly lying positions – would eventually be cut off and lost. In turn, this would further reduce the forces available for the defence of the next line of vulnerable, yet technically defensible, positions of strategic importance.

By the early hours of the morning of 23 February, Bapst, having weighed up all the options, concluded that a tactical withdrawal was infinitely preferable to the needless obliteration of valuable and redeployable units. After lengthy consultations with General Chrétien, who ultimately decided to leave the decision to the man on the spot, Bapst took the bold option of abandoning Brabant. Needless to say, the implications of this were severe – not least for Bapst himself – and the order was not given lightly, especially because Bapst had little reliable information about the broader situation across the front. He was able to make only an educated guess as to the actual strategic significance of Brabant at this moment.

Nevertheless, a French withdrawal from Brabant was executed

efficiently and with few losses. But the decision instantly created controversy. Almost immediately the move began to appear premature when
reinforcements unexpectedly reached General Chrétien at his command
post at Fort Souville. Thereafter, Brabant's strategic importance as a
northerly lying French stronghold seemed to rise as, simultaneously, the
need to redeploy the men who had held it lessened. Chrétien now began
to waver about the wisdom of Bapst's decision and, for some hours, could
not decide whether to let it stand or countermand it. A response to this
territorial forfeit from the Central Armies Group Headquarters – in effect,
General Herr's hierarchical chiefs – seems to have settled his mind. It
stated:

> Every defence point must be held, even when overrun or surrounded.
> Such resistance, no matter how hopeless or futile it may seem, may have in-
> calculable consequences, serving to slow up the enemy advance or to
> facilitate our counterattack.

Thereafter, Chrétien informed Bapst – rather unfairly in the light of what
he had said earlier – that the area 'should not have been evacuated without
the permission of the superior command'. Therefore, he ordered that 'the
General commanding the 72nd Division [i.e. Bapst] will take measures to
reoccupy Brabant'.

But as is so often the case with military orders handed down, the
wording of the despatch – straightforward and to the point – did not
betray the sheer magnitude of the task in hand. In fact, this was an almost
impossible one given the prevailing circumstances, and made all the more
difficult by a postscript relayed to Bapst informing him not to overcommit
himself, in men or resources, during the attempted re-occupation. With
his scope for manoeuvre effectively curtailed, Bapst nevertheless set about
raising a force. An already absurd situation now descended further into
farce, however, as it became clear that there was not even a handful of fit
and able men readily available to him. It was only after this depressing
information reached Chrétien that a measure of reality took hold and the
plan to retake Brabant finally abandoned. The desolated village, left abandoned overnight, was seized by the Germans late the next morning. The
initial French front line was now all but theirs.

4

Fort Douaumont

What passing-bells for those who die as cattle?
Only the monstrous anger of the guns.
Only the stuttering rifles' rapid rattle
Can patter out their hasty orisons.
Wilfred Owen, *Anthem for Doomed Youth*

WHEREVER THEY COULD and whenever it was possible, the French generals at Verdun continued to command small counterstrokes against the marauding German infantry. These usually proved to be pointless missions. In purely human terms, however, their effects were disastrous, with the perpetual slaughter of their comrades leading to a slow but steady decline in morale among the *poilus*.

Yet, conversely, such measures led to similar demoralization, albeit less marked, setting in among the German troops. To a small extent, the attacking infantry was being ground down by the ferocity of a resistance that they had been led to believe would not even exist once they stepped on to the battlefield. Similarly, the High Command was somewhat perplexed by such a turn of events and, in the words of Horne, this 'had the effect of persuading the Germans to greater prudence', though nothing less than a cautious approach was to be expected from Falkenhayn.

More pertinently perhaps, the expected breakthrough – which, in view of the strategic and tactical balance of affairs across the battle zone, could not be far off – was still to materialize. French forces, everywhere under siege and attack by a vastly superior opponent, would not yield. Their tenacity and heroism in the face of an unprecedented onslaught were so far managing to stave off absolute French ruin at Verdun.

The German attack quickly began to lose the element of surprise upon which it so depended. Whether this was as a result of sheer repetition cannot be determined. Certainly, the rapidity of the artillery barrage began to reduce, if for no other reason than such a high level of shelling could not be sustained for long. But there were other practical manifestations of the fact that the French infantry were getting to know what to expect from the Germans. As early as 23 February, for example, methods

An aerial shot following Fort Douaumont in outline

for successfully avoiding the consequences of the flame-thrower were put into practice by the *poilus*.

Still, the French defence was not yet operating at full capacity. The infantry was constantly being pushed back and forced to improvise. The artillery was each day becoming slightly more effective but this did not amount to much when most of what was fired veered off target or, worse, failed to reach the enemy line. More crucially, the lack of general preparation before the onslaught was beginning to tell. Severed communications lines could not be replaced nor could support lines be used, for they simply did not exist. Where they had not been cut by the German artillery, road and rail links functioned poorly and suffered from overcrowding, mismanagement, and poor servicing. Those few supply lines that were operational were being stretched to the limit. For a multitude of reasons, encompassing all of the above, reinforcements could not be moved up the line, and so those forces at the front received neither desperately needed aid nor replenishment.

The Germans continued to progress in the general direction of Verdun. The last major point held by the French along what had been their first line was the Bois d'Herbebois. According to one French infantryman present, the front here had been methodically reduced to 'a number of crumbling ditches and shell-holes which had once been a trench'. After the usual defensive obstinacy, the area fell in the course of the third day of the battle. With the possession of Haumont to the north-west, the Bois des Caures to the north, and now Herbebois to the north-east, the

Germans engulfed the next point of strategic importance, the village of Beaumont, inching ever closer to Verdun as they did. It fell on 24 February.

Increasingly, the Germans were paying for each new advance with more men dead. Their losses were still minor compared to those being suffered by the French – it was not unusual for them to lose whole units at a time – but, all the same, this dissipation of their infantry had not been bargained for nor did it auger well. Furthermore, those on both sides that had survived since the start of the battle were slowly being overcome by physical exhaustion.

The series of disasters that had blighted the French since the opening of the campaign arguably reached its nadir during the night of 23–4 February at the village of Samogneux. The fighting around this location had been especially intense, some of the worst seen so far. The German determination to advance was matched by stubborn French resistance that saw every step of ground being defended to the death.

The scene was one of carnage. A French lieutenant described how:

> Every particle of ground on which we stood [at Samogneux] was searched by the enemy's fire – the front, the supply line, the rear, the crests, the hollows, the roads, the village, the bridges and the stations – the hills around us smoked like volcanoes. Every second and with every step new holes opened in the shell-torn ground . . .

The defending force had been hemmed in by the VII Reserve Corps, fresh from victory at Haumont and eager to add to their conquests. Their attack, and the searing artillery fire, remained constant. Meanwhile, French reinforcements headed for Samogneux, and were annihilated on their way up the line. Such was the devastation being wrought that all cohesiveness was battered out of the French force and, after a while, there was little recognizable leadership on the spot.

Those *poilus* not yet dead wandered around exposed and in a state of confusion, searching out any sort of shelter however insufficient it may have been. Somehow the rumour spread that Samogneux had, in fact, fallen. When this information reached General Bapst he sought confirmation of the situation. A lieutenant-colonel at Samogneux verified that he was still holding the position, but added, 'I shall be doing the impossible if I keep you informed of events'.

This was the last that Bapst heard for some hours. By late evening he had become convinced that, in view of the intensity of the attack on Samogneux and the silence from there, the position must indeed have fallen. He immediately commanded its recapture, and troops were despatched in the direction of the village. In the mean time, French artillery batteries – acting under the directions of the command at Verdun which was working under the assumption that the spot was now in German hands – were ordered to target the area. A little after midnight, a two-hour barrage was directed against Samogneux. There was no let-up because, for almost the first time at the Battle of Verdun, the French heavy guns began firing with remarkable accuracy and great efficiency. The defenders were obliterated by their own shell fire. There was no way out of the inferno for the French infantry. The Germans, equally perplexed and delighted at the situation they saw unfolding before them, simply waited for the shelling to subside. An hour after it did they walked into Samogneux. Meanwhile, General Bapst's 72nd Division which, according to one of its number, was from early on 'quite resigned to the prospect of extinction', ceased to exist as a fighting force, having lost in four days of fighting nearly 10,000 men and 192 officers.

German superiority in the battle was now established beyond doubt. Perhaps unknowingly, they had all but smashed through the belatedly established intermediary line, which ran through Beaumont and Samogneux, between France's first and second defensive positions. So encouraged were the attackers by this success that none other than the Kaiser himself was persuaded to pay a visit to the Fifth Army's new headquarters at Stenay. He wished to observe for himself the fall of Verdun which, it was believed, was no more than a day or two away at the most.

Historical consensus suggests that 24 February 1916 was the day when the dam burst at Verdun, the moment when the German forces finally broke the back of the stout defence. Once the intermediary line had been violated, there was little standing in the way of the Germans as they descended upon the second French defensive line to the north of Douaumont. Everything, it seems, had been expended by the French in attempting to stem the irresistible advance of the enemy: men, materials, even hope.

All day the German artillery pounded away at the French positions. Vast gaps now existed in the depleted French line but little or nothing could be done to address the situation because there were not enough men to fill the holes. Where reservists could be called upon they proved to be inadequate. The 37th African Division, for example, was moved in to replace the obliterated 72nd. Reputedly one of the best and most feared units in all of the French Army, these colonial soldiers simply did not know what had hit them once placed into the fray. With little experience of situations such as the one they now faced at Verdun, and no adequate preparations to equip them to cope with the ordeal, the division was instantly stunned into submission by the ferocity of the German attack. Some were frozen to the spot with fear, others turned and ran only to be mown down by merciless machine-gun fire.

Other reservists were mortally wounded without ever engaging in battle. Soon, the supply of soldiers was utterly exhausted. Across the battle zone, many men were left leaderless while others roamed aimlessly in a trance-like state. Disorder was everywhere apparent, and compounded by the reality that there was a dearth of guns and insufficient ammunition to service those pieces that could be used. Meanwhile, the Germans rolled through the gaps in the French line, with von Lockow's Brandenburgers heading in the direction of Fort Douaumont.

The day was a total disaster for the French, the worst yet experienced at Verdun. As valuable resources (including artillery) dwindled, integral communication points were lost (a number of bridges across the River Meuse were cut), and everywhere the line pressed back, morale throughout the force plummeted to new depths. It was no surprise, then, when the inadequately bulwarked second line – under constant attack for so long – crumbled in the course of the afternoon. It now appeared that Verdun was shortly to be taken.

Later in the day, General Balfourier's XX Corps reached the Verdun zone but, tired and hungry after an arduous trek, could not be deployed immediately. Balfourier relieved General Chrétien who had witnessed the enemy make more gains in one day of the battle than they had managed in the previous three. For the first time in eighteen months, there was genuine movement along the Western Front, and no tangible block existed between the probing German forces and Verdun. A march on the city at this moment was barred only by disparate and dispirited huddles of men, often stuck in overcrowded dug-outs or isolated pockets, exposed and up to their knees in mud. They appeared not as an intrepid fighting force but rather as a bedraggled bunch of war refugees who had accidentally stumbled on to a battlefield. The best that these men could offer by way of viable resistance was through hand-to-hand combat which afforded good opportunity for venting the frustrations attached to imminent defeat. For suddenly, in the space of a day, this seemed to be what fate had in store for them.

Counter-moves, however, now more pointless than ever during the late afternoon and evening of 24 February, continued to be demanded of the remaining infantry by their generals. From wherever they stood, the *poilus* persisted in sniping at the enemy. The German infantry was thus forced to stay on its guard.

The action was now focused around Fort Douaumont. Supposedly the strongest single fortress in the world at the time, the fort at Douaumont

Fort Douaumont

Fort Douaumont had been designed to be the centrepiece of the fortified defensive network in front of the city of Verdun, and it became a symbol of the fortunes of the two armies engaged in the Meuse region in 1916. Its vast size and great military capacity also meant that it remained a key feature of the Battle of Verdun and gave to whoever possessed it an advantage that was difficult to negate.

Located some 6 kilometres to the north-east of Verdun, at an altitude of 395 metres, the position offered excellent observation of the surrounding countryside. Begun in 1885, the polygonal fort was continually upgraded until shortly before the outbreak of World War I. It was encased in a thick layer of protective concrete, the interior was always dark and damp, and it provided only a few basic necessities for those garrisoned there. An intricate labyrinth of tunnels linked the fort's system of armaments which featured: a 75-mm gun post to the front of the position; a 155-mm gun turret on the right flank; two machine-gun emplacements; and five armoured look-out posts.

Before 1916, Fort Douaumont was widely believed to be inviolable and, though never severely tested, events in the war to that date did little to disprove the notion. Separate enemy attacks – in November 1914 and March 1915 – had left the fort largely unscathed. In the aftermath of the collapse of the Belgian forts in 1914, however, French military strategists lost faith in fixed fortifications. Consequently, Douaumont was included in the general down-grading of all French-held fortifications in late 1915 and stripped of the majority of its 400-strong garrison.

The reduced force stationed within Fort Douaumont was caught unawares when, on 25 February 1916, the III Brandenburgers over-ran the position. Not a single shot was fired in defence of supposedly one of the strongest fortresses in the world. The loss was immediately recognized by the French as a severe one though no one could calculate just how costly it would prove. The Germans, on the other hand, could hardly comprehend the ease with which they had captured the fort, and celebrated a victory which many thought pre-destined the ultimate collapse of France as a fighting force.

An immediate attempt to recapture Douaumont ended in bloody failure. Thereafter, the Germans exploited to the hilt their occupancy of the bulwark, inflicting substantial damages upon those French forces located in its vicinity. Fighting, meanwhile, continued in the local area throughout the spring and summer months. In May, an explosion within the fortress – caused when a munitions' dump caught fire – killed hundreds of German troops and undermined the strength of the force stationed there. General Mangin tried to exploit this situation but a formidable French offensive on the 22 May failed to dislodge the Germans, showing that the latter could still claim supremacy across the Verdun battle zone.

It was only after the fighting initiative had swung firmly in favour of the French that they could mount a serious counter-move to try to reclaim the fort. On 24 October, as part of the general offensive against the German positions in front of Verdun, Fort Douaumont was retaken with almost as much ease as it had been in February. The German command, though, mindful of the bulwark's capability, kept its artillery fixed upon the fortress for some time to come, thereby ensuring that Fort Douaumont could not be used against their retreating forces.

Plan of Fort Douamont

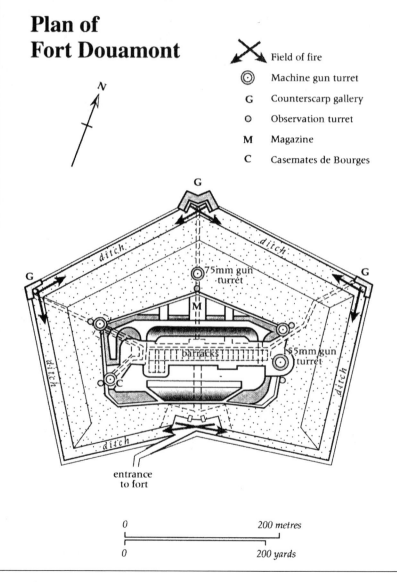

Fort Douaumont in 1916

Gun emplacement atop Fort Douaumont

was an enormous polygonal structure that served as a cornerstone for the entire Verdun defensive system. The novelist Henry Bordeaux (also an official French chronicler of the Battle of Verdun) commented that Fort Douaumont was 'like some incubus weighing upon the whole surrounding countryside'. Certainly, it seemed to be highly significant, and the Germans believed it posed a great threat that needed to be overcome.

Begun in 1885, the fort was in a seemingly constant state of construction and up-date, and building work on it ceased only in 1913. A protective layer of concrete, varying from 2.5 metres thick at its widest on the western side to 1.5 metres on the eastern side, was designed to withstand the most forceful of artillery attacks. Fort Douaumont was constructed with a number of outward-looking armed posts, and featured a retractable 155-mm and two 75-mm gun turrets. Further, two machine-gun turrets and five armoured look-out posts were all linked by a series of underground tunnels.

Within, the construction was a veritable labyrinth of tunnels and passageways (featuring chicanes for fighting at close quarters) off which lay dark, damp chambers of varying size. While much planning had gone into the defensive and military aspects of the fortress, little thought seems to have been given to the conditions within it which were, at best, rudimentary. Ventilation was a persistent problem, with air often in short supply. The sanitary arrangements, too, left a lot to be desired. There were no toilets within the fort, and waste had to be disposed of in the grounds outside, hardly an adequate arrangement in peacetime but, during a battle, it was partially or even wholly untenable. During the height of the conflict, the stench within the fort was sometimes so severe that troops were overcome with nausea. Neither was there a fitted electricity supply. Lighting was provided by candles or gas-lamp, warmth – and it was always cold inside the fort – by fires.

The fortress was situated at an altitude of 395 metres and, with its sweeping panorama of the surrounding woods and ravines, it offered excellent surveillance in every direction and for kilometres around. So far, any German infantry moves towards the position had been comfortably thwarted by the fort's guns, and the enemy's artillery shells, which had been raining down on the structure since 21 February, had had little impact on its overall capacities.

Nevertheless, despite all the myths and accolades declaring Fort Douaumont's impregnability, the position fell on 25 February with a minimum of German losses. It is not entirely clear how a handful of pioneering German assault troops managed to capture the fortress without a struggle. Various accounts claim to tell the heroic story of how one of the most powerful fortresses on Earth was taken. By far the most creditable of these centres around the exploits of a Sergeant Kunze of the III Corps.

The Brandenburgers' general order for 25 February was to advance across the woodlands to the north of Fort Douaumont. The detachment that Sergeant Kunze was a member of found the command particularly easy to follow because it was marching into the gap created by the collapse

The view from Fort Douaumont with the ossuary visible in the distance

of the 37th African Division. Not so much as a shot was fired in anger directly at the advancing Germans as they closed in on the northerly approaches to the fort. Once there, they noticed how a series of breaches had been opened in the barbed-wire entanglements that surrounded the fort. These were easily cut through using wire cutters but the next step, of crossing Douaumont's deep defensive ditch, proved far more problematic. Fortunately for Kunze, the heavy fall-out from a shell landing close to where he stood propelled him into the moat. A little shaken but unhurt, he beckoned the rest of his detachment to follow him into the gully. Forming a human pyramid enabled Kunze to push his way into one of the fort's galleries. He then let his comrades in through a steel door but were cautious and only two chose to follow him.

Once within the fort, Kunze and his companions proceeded to explore the surprisingly empty tunnels within the bunker. Reaching the 155-mm gun turret, which was firing at the time, Kunze, now alone, disarmed it thereby preventing further damage being inflicted upon German forces advancing to the east of the fort. He arrested two French gunners, who duly escaped, but a roomful of the French garrison was captured when the wily sergeant simply locked them inside the chamber they had assembled in to receive a briefing. This was to be the extent of Kunze's valiant

Fort Douaumont's fixed 155 mm gun

endeavours, however. Stumbling across a room full of freshly prepared food – something he had not seen for some months – he succumbed to temptation and sat down to eat.

Meanwhile, quite independently of Kunze, other units of Germans had entered the fortress. A Lieutenant Radtke had made a similarly brave, though arguably easier, passage into the fort. Together with about twenty men, Radtke stunned three French infantrymen who, immediately upon being captured and to the lieutenant's amazement, revealed that the entire garrison at Fort Douaumont comprised no more than sixty men. Minutes later, a Captain Haupt arrested the guardian of the fort, the elderly Chenot.

When these various parties met, the defence of the fort against a possible French counter-move was organized along tenable military lines. In the mean time, every Frenchman garrisoned at Fort Douaumont had been rounded up and taken prisoner. Between them, they had failed to fire a single shot in defence of the bulwark.

Why the Germans found Douaumont in a state of such utter defence-lessness is curious. At the outbreak of the war, Fort Douaumont had a fixed garrison of some 500 men and six officers. But, as we have seen, after the collapse of the Belgian forts in 1914, French military thinking soon decreed stationary fortifications to be outmoded and something of a liability. When, in 1915, Joffre ordered the down-grading of all forts, Douaumont was left with a skeleton garrison of fifty-six men, enough it was thought to man the 155-mm, 75-mm, and other gun emplacements.

Indeed, in 1916, the forts were held in such low esteem that, as soon as the RFV came under attack in February, the order was given to abandon and demolish Fort Douaumont. By the time of its capture, this command had yet to be carried out, possibly because one of General Chrétien's last acts was to countermand this instruction and demand that the fort be defended 'to the last'. To this end, he enacted plans to send a reinforcing garrison to Douaumont.

Amid much confusion, no one was really sure of the true state of Fort Douaumont's defensive capabilities. Some believed that it was abandoned or on the point of abandonment. Others thought it had been reinforced and was therefore 'safe'. Albeit unwittingly, the Brandenburgers had merely exploited the situation, achieving the *coup* of the campaign up to this point. Undoubtedly, they were aided by the fact that the garrison holding Douaumont was, by 25 February, completely demoralized by the harrowing effects of four days' worth of 420-mm enemy shells pounding the fort and reverberating through it. Indeed, so shell-shocked were they that they had retired to the lower level of the fort, leaving the upper levels largely deserted.

The ease with which the Germans had captured the fort aroused suspicions that they had walked into some kind of deadly trap or time-bomb. But the notion was soon dispelled. At this stage, the French were incapable of such trickery. The attacking force had bought the prize of Fort Douaumont for the price of thirty-two dead that day. Later calculations suggested that, for the French over the next eight months, the cost of the fort's loss ran into tens of thousands dead.

At the headquarters of the Fifth Army the initial response to the news that the fort had been taken was utter disbelief. This did not stop the Germans from acting with characteristic swiftness in consolidating the gain, however. That very night, under cover of the artillery, supplies,

men, and enough ammunition to ensure that the fort's weapons could
be kept going for a considerable time, were shipped into the bulwark
via its underground tunnel entrances. Almost immediately, the 75-
mm and 155-mm guns were turned on those French troops still in the
vicinity of Douaumont. Thereafter, they fired continuously for days at
a time.

Though unexpected, the victory was undoubtedly a decisive one and
was heralded throughout Germany as such. Most commentators felt that,
in all likelihood, it was the harbinger of ultimate German triumph, an
event that would bring the end of the war in the west significantly closer.
In the light of Douaumont's repute everywhere, it is easy to understand
such optimism throughout Germany and the German military.

Despite prevailing military thinking, the French immediately recognized the loss as a major blow, especially in terms of morale and battle
strategy. The French nation was shocked by the news. Most simply could
not comprehend what had happened. In his memoirs of the Battle of
Verdun, Pétain wrote:

> . . . we had lost the best and most modern of our earth-works, the tangible
> expression of our reasons for confidence, the lofty observation point from
> which we should have been able to survey and sweep the ground over
> which the Germans must advance, and from which the enemy would now
> be able to spy upon us and direct his attacks on the remotest corners of the
> consecrated battle field of Verdun.

A sense of panic quickly spread throughout the French line. At the front,
the *poilus* began to lose all hope. Many now pondered on the wisdom of
the sacrifices so needlessly extracted from their ranks over the past few
days. Among the generals, who were mostly dumbfounded by the reversal, recrimination was instant, yet no one could begin to answer how this
catastrophe had been allowed to come about.

In Verdun itself, a general evacuation of the city's remaining civilian
population was ordered. Many people were reluctant to leave their
homes, businesses, and belongings and, in some cases, the *sous-préfet* had to
ask for police assistance to get people to leave. The city's public records
were sent to the relative safety of Bar-le-Duc, some 50 kilometres to the
south-west of Verdun, and jurisdiction handed over to the military.
Verdun was left as a ghost town, with only three elders permitted to stay
behind in a symbolically defiant gesture. These men helped run a canteen
for soldiers.

Thereafter, the city's function was a purely military one. Long-range
German artillery guns ravaged much of its centre over the course of the

battle, but the Citadel – which stands bunker-like in the city centre – remained immune to such attacks. It continued to be utilized as an effective command centre for the entire French logistical operation at Verdun, doubling as a convenient stop-off point for troops on their way to the front. The Citadel's sheer enormity was its strength. It could house as many as 10,000 men at a time, and was fully equipped with a communications' network, a munitions' hold, a vast kitchen, and a bakery (which could produce up to 30,000 loaves a day for the Verdun force). It also provided recreational entertainment within its sturdy walls for battle-weary officers and soldiers.

With the loss of Fort Douaumont, the Citadel in many respects took over as 'the tangible expression of our reasons for confidence' at Verdun. After inspecting the Citadel in early March 1916, a visiting dignitary, René Benjamin, wrote: 'It stood, a vast forbidding mass, and before each of its entrances, deep in shadow, were artillery-men, armed and helmeted. A stirring sight.' Such sentiment served to disguise the débâcle of Douaumont for some months to come.

On the other hand, the German celebrations were vociferous and lengthy. Such a stunning and unexpected victory was believed to portend the ultimate collapse of the French forces at Verdun and, indeed, along the Western Front more generally. The *Frankfurt Gazette* announced: 'It was the only great and almost impregnable fort at Verdun. The hardest part of our task is accomplished: henceforth there will be nothing but the remorseless progress of an elemental force'. Meanwhile, in attempting to capitalize fully on the declining morale that the Germans were now sure must be affecting the French before Verdun, aircraft littered the French line with leaflets that read: 'Douaumont has fallen. All will soon be over. Don't let yourselves be killed for nothing.'

Perhaps it would soon all be over. France's darkest hour of the whole German assault on Verdun had arrived. On the night of 25–6 February, there seemed nothing to stop the German Fifth Army taking the entire Verdun zone. It looked as though Falkenhayn's plan to administer a fatal blow to the French at Verdun, by bleeding the enemy force there, lay in tatters and that the Crown Prince would actually succeed in capturing the fortress, thereby only striking a stunning moral blow upon the French nation. The Crown Prince himself recognized that he was 'in fact, within a stone's throw of victory!'

But, at this very moment, fortune unexpectedly favoured the beleaguered French. There was to be no final push on Verdun that night because, amazingly, the Germans had exhausted their reserves, and those forces in the breach were in a state of considerable fatigue. The Crown Prince recalled how he had, at this time:

General de Castlenau at Verdun

. . . no reserves left for the immediate and energetic exploitation of our first successes, and the troops, who had been fighting uninterruptedly for four days, found the task beyond their strength. So the psychological moment passed unutilised.

The grand scheme for a deadly war of attrition, then, had won a reprieve, inadvertently or otherwise. How long this would last depended, of course, on the next French move and on the Crown Prince's ability to bring into the battle fresh units of troops.

The time had long since been reached when only affirmative action from on high could save the French forces at Verdun from a humiliating defeat. On the face of it, nothing short of a miracle would now suffice. It was surely only a matter of time before the attacking forces regrouped and the advance upon Verdun was resumed.

Salvation of a sort arrived shortly after dawn on 25 February, when General de Castlenau swept into Verdun. John Keegan has observed that de Castlenau 'saw the fight for Verdun as a test of his country's capacity to sustain the defence of the national territory and keep alive the hope of ultimate victory'. Consequently, he was horrified by the early reports that reached his desk concerning the conduct of the first few days of the battle. He decided to act and, having first obtained from Joffre plenipotentiary powers, headed for the battle zone. Although he arrived far too late to try to prevent the fall of Fort Douaumont, he nevertheless began immediately to utilize his authority in the most forthright manner.

Noel Joseph Edouard de Curiéres de Castlenau was of aristocratic stock. Born in the Pyrénées region on Christmas Eve 1851, he came from a distinguished line of French generals. A Castlenau had fought alongside Napoleon at the start of the nineteenth century, and another had been with Napoleon III when he capitulated at Sedan in 1870. The family were staunch Roman Catholics, and de Castlenau was neither ashamed of this heritage nor afraid to proclaim his religious convictions. Undoubtedly, though, in the avowedly Republican ranks of the army in which he served, such a stance did nothing to further his military career.

Of diminutive and portly stature, he was a most able and intelligent soldier, a fine tactician and renowned staff officer. In a more meritocratic service there is little doubt that de Castlenau would have achieved higher office than he did. After a full military education – and later a stint at the War College – he fought in the Franco-Prussian War, and thereafter served with distinction in the line and as a staff officer. But his beliefs – which were never far from the surface – continually stirred up trouble, causing embarrassment for the upper echelons of the army and making de Castlenau enemies among left-leaning political groups. It came as no surprise when, in 1900, he was convicted, along with two fellow officers, of expressing anti-Dreyfusian sentiment and purged from the General Staff.

For some years he wallowed in the relative obscurity of Nancy, commanding an infantry regiment there. It was only in 1911 that he returned to the centre stage, when Joffre – inexperienced in the more specialized aspects of staff work – made him his immediate deputy. De Castlenau's family and religious backgrounds still working against him, the appointment was a controversial one, but his influence on French war planning was paramount. He played a significant role in the framing of Plan XVII, persuaded Joffre to enact the 1913 Conscription Bill, and spent the three years immediately before the war liaising with the British Army staff.

Early on, his outlook on World War I was coloured by the loss in action of three of his sons, and also by the experience of commanding the Second Army at Nancy in 1914. A strong advocate of the offensive, at the outbreak of the war he led his force in a north-easterly direction, only to be pushed back by the Germans. Nevertheless, his force defended Nancy valiantly, and de Castlenau oversaw the successful securing of the most

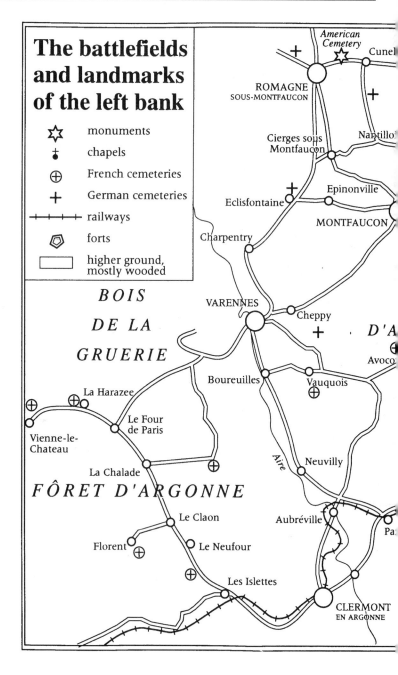

The battlefields and landmarks of the left bank

☆ monuments

⚲ chapels

⊕ French cemeteries

✝ German cemeteries

┼┼┼┼┼ railways

⬠ forts

▭ higher ground, mostly wooded

American Cemetery Cunel

ROMAGNE SOUS-MONTFAUCON

✝

Cierges sous Montfaucon   Nantillo

Epinonville

Eclisfontaine   ✝

MONTFAUCON

Charpentry

BOIS   VARENNES   Cheppy

DE LA   *D'A*

GRUERIE   Avoco

Boureuilles   Vauquois

La Harazee

⊕ ⊕   Le Four de Paris

Vienne-le-Chateau

Neuvilly

La Chalade   ⊕

FÔRET D'ARGONNE

Le Claon   Aubréville   Pa

Florent ⊕   Le Neufour

⊕   Les Islettes

CLERMONT EN ARGONNE

5   The battlefield and landmarks of the left bank

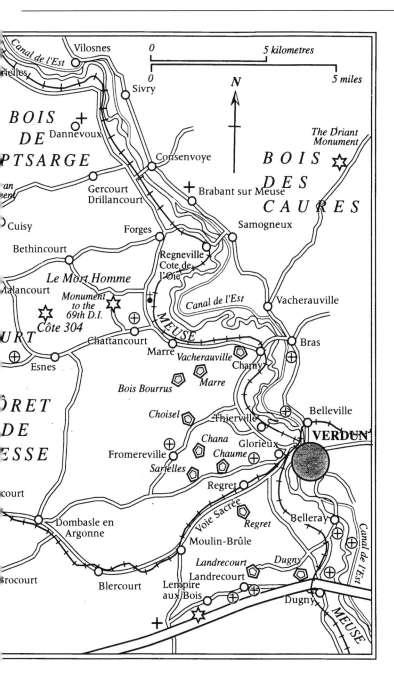

BOIS
DE
PTSARGE

Vilosnes

Canal de l'Est

delles

Sivry

0   5 kilometres

0   5 miles

N

Dannevoux

Consenvoye

BOIS
DES
CAURES

The Driant
Monument

an
en

Gercourt
Drillancourt

Brabant sur Meuse

Cuisy

Forges

Samogneux

Bethincourt

Regneville
Cote de
l'Oie

Le Mort Homme

Malancourt

Monument
to the
69th D.I.

Côte 304

Canal de l'Est

Vacherauville

URT

Chattancourt

Marre

Esnes

Vacherauville

Bras

Bois Bourrus

Marre

Charny

RET
DE
ESSE

Choisel

Thierville

Belleville

Chana

Fromereville

Sartelles

Chaume

Glorieux

VERDUN

court

Regret

Voie Sacrée

Belleray

Dombasle en
Argonne

Regret

Moulin-Brûle

Dugny

Landrecourt

rocourt

Blercourt

Landrecourt
Lempire
aux Bois

Dugny

MEUSE

Canal de l'Est

easterly portion of the French line. In turn, this was to help facilitate the French victory at the Marne.

In 1915, de Castlenau was appointed commander of the Central Armies Group, and was responsible for conducting the main offensive moves that year at Artois and Champagne. By December, he was back at general headquarters as Joffre's Chief of Staff. This was a blatantly political appointment, made under the exigencies of war, and designed to curb Joffre's more adventurous, and increasingly less trustworthy, side.

Instantly, Verdun became an issue of some concern to de Castlenau. Unlike many of his peers, from a relatively early stage, he seems to have taken seriously the supposed enemy threat to this section of the front. It was he who visited the region in January 1916, ordering that all defensive works be concentrated upon the right bank of the Meuse, and commanding the construction of the intermediary line of defence. Arguably, it was only as a consequence of this most recent work that de Castlenau was in a position to return to Verdun a month later, the Germans having been critically slowed in their advance because of the reinforced right-bank defences.

On arrival at Verdun, the General wasted no time in setting to work, surveying the front and considering the state of the sector's defensive positions. His decisiveness was a breath of fresh air to the battle-weary command at Verdun. He was immediately able to instil fresh hope and a semblance of order to proceedings. He quickly became convinced that Verdun could be saved. He recognized that the right bank must be held, and published an order to that effect in the early morning of 25 February. It stated: 'There can be no question of any other course than of checking the enemy, cost what it may, on that bank'.

Taking a longer-term view, de Castlenau decided that, if France was ultimately to defeat the Germans at Verdun, it had little option other than to extend its defences to the vulnerable left bank. To oversee this most arduous of tasks, the entire Second Army, held in reserve since the start of the year, was to be brought up to the Verdun front. The commander of the Second, Henri-Philippe Pétain, was to be entrusted with responsibility for the entire defence of Verdun, on both banks of the River Meuse.

The choice was almost certainly made from necessity because of the circumstances of the war. To some extent, Pétain was simply in the right place at the right time though he undoubtedly had the required capabilities for undertaking a task of such magnitude. Nevertheless, it was a slightly strange decision, if for no other reason than that Pétain was one of the few officers in the French Army at this time who openly and consistently questioned the guiding philosophies of the General Staff. He considered the idea of continually attacking, regardless of cost and strategic implications, to constitute folly of the highest order. Furthermore, he did not believe that the needless loss of life caused in this way could be in any way justified. He was on record as saying, 'firepower kills; artillery should be used to gain ground, and infantry to occupy it'. Consequently, Pétain was not the General Staff's favourite son. He had clashed with de Castlenau over the conduct of the 1915 offensives, and others before him. But his talents could not be seriously doubted, and he commanded the respect of the *poilus* who admired his independence of mind and that he clearly valued them as individuals rather than seeing them as an anonymous and expendable mass of cannon fodder.

Some historians have suggested, perhaps unfairly, that Pétain's outlook was conditioned by the fact that he was 'not a fighter by temperament'. Whether this was true or not, it was certainly a view shared by his superiors, and goes some way to accounting for why in 1914, a little less than two years before he was due to retire, he remained a colonel. Nevertheless, his eye for defence meant that he was suited for the job, and the appointment was not a complete surprise, least of all to Pétain, who had already sent a delegation of his staff to Verdun a few days earlier to assess the situation on the ground.

Alistair Horne was one of the first to expound the theory that:

> De Castlenau's snap decision [to defend Verdun on both banks of the Meuse] was one that in its fateful implications would affect not merely the course of the Battle of Verdun, or even of the war itself, but also the whole stream of subsequent French history.

Despite its seeming bombast, there is more than just a grain of truth in this statement. If a sinister trap had been set by the German High Command, then de Castlenau decided to take the French Army headlong into it. As Falkenhayn had predicted in his memorandum to the Kaiser, France had set itself on a course for defending the symbolic position at Verdun whatever the cost. At this juncture, de Castlenau – or someone else – could have given Verdun up as a lost cause, and drawn the French line into a retreat back beyond the city and on to the difficult terrain there, where the Germans could not have hoped to advance easily or cheaply. But this would not happen: the 'bleeding' process, as Falkenhayn had envisioned it, could now begin.

The 'attack without respite' having faltered, the Germans had lost the opportunity to push on to Verdun sooner rather than later. Yet conceivably, this might have been a deliberate ploy by Falkenhayn – holding back vital resources and men at a point when they were most needed – to ensure that his macabre plan, which he was determined to see put into operation, could ultimately unfold.

An air of unreality now clung to all that was happening at Verdun. The French force continued in a state of turmoil, especially at the front. Despite all de Castlenau's efforts, little could be done to reverse the effects of the heavy losses suffered so far. Moreover, though the German infantry was in temporary standstill, the artillery kept up its frightful barrage, the higher-calibre guns in particular wreaking dreadful havoc. One French captain, in the Douaumont area, noted that, 'The rate of firing [at this time] was such that as soon as a shell made a hole another fell next to it and filled it in. In some places the ground looked like the surface of a storm-tossed sea.'

Pétain, meanwhile, had to be tracked down. He was discovered late at night in Paris in the company of his mistress. Taken immediately the next morning to see Joffre at his headquarters at Chantilly, he was told simply to save Verdun.

The turbulent day of 25 February passed. The Kaiser left Stenay that evening without having witnessed the fall of Verdun and the triumphant march of his son's army into the city. Nevertheless, he must have felt sure that he would be returning in the very near future to witness such a procession.

5

The Hell of Verdun

One does not fight with men against material;
it is with material served by men that one makes war.
Henri-Philippe Pétain

BEFORE WORLD WAR I, Henri-Philippe Pétain's military career had been beset with contention and, consequently, was hardly a distinguished one. In the years up to 1914, he had about him the air of a journeyman soldier. He was disliked for his obstinacy and widely resented by his peers for his views but cared not a jot about either. Born on 24 April 1856 near Arras in the northern French *département* of Pas de Calais, Pétain came from a poor peasant family and was orphaned at an early age. Educated at military school, he graduated in 1878 before embarking upon a long infantry career in France, serving mostly with the *Chasseurs Alpin* along the Italian frontier, before spending periods in Besançon, Marseilles, and Paris.

Promotion came only slowly to Pétain, and it did not help that he insisted on staying in France when the colonial services offered brighter prospects to a man of his disposition and ability. In 1890 he was a captain but, over the course of the next decade, rose only to the rank of major. He had no influential friends of note nor any obvious religious or political affiliations though he did have a slight anti-Dreyfusian outlook. In other respects, however, he was a most controversial figure. Though seemingly a cold character of few words, he had a fiery nature and, over the years, clashed notably and on repeated occasions with his military superiors. Similarly, he did little to endear himself to politicians. He once famously told Raymond Poincaré that 'nobody was better placed than the President himself to be aware that France was neither led nor governed'. It was a trait that did nothing to further his career.

In the early 1900s, Pétain began to concern himself more with military theory and tactics, largely through closer associations with the War College. Yet it would seem that he was forever out of step with contemporary military trends in France, expressing defensive doctrines when all around him were thinking in terms of the offensive. His stance earned him much recognition, however, if only because he was forever swimming against the tide. But the majority remained unconvinced, his notions did not prevail, and, prior to the outbreak of hostilities in 1914, he appeared to be heading for retirement and a quiet life.

Then the war intervened. In the first month of the conflict he was put in temporary charge of a brigade of the Fifth Army. Thus afforded the opportunity to shine as a natural leader of men, he distinguished himself, first at Charleroi, then at the Battle of the Guise. This won him the rank of Brigadier-General and the command of his own division which was to play a part in the offensive at the Marne. What was by now, by his own standards at least, a meteoric rise continued when he took over command of the XXXII Corps near his birthplace close to Arras.

His motto was 'victory at the smallest cost', and he was appalled when he led his Corps in the offensive at Artois in 1915, even though he saw some success by taking the Vimy Ridge before the offensive became bogged down. By the time of the Champagne offensive later that year, he was commander of the Second Army. His experience at Champagne, coupled with what he had seen earlier at Artois, merely served to reinforce his view that the only way for the infantry to advance was in the aftermath of heavy artillery work, with the process then being repeated only after small gains had been made and properly consolidated. He believed that the only means of defeating the Germans was by wearing them down in a piecemeal fashion, and that emphasis should be placed on expending materials rather than men. He outlined his ideas in a report to Joffre at the end of 1915 but the latter remained singularly unimpressed.

Still, his tenets remained unyielding, and he brought them to bear on events at Verdun in 1916. In the aftermath of de Castlenau's judgements about bulwarking the right- and the left-bank defences, it is clear that Pétain was tactically restricted when he took up the assignment. He had no other remit than that handed down to him by the General Staff. As a commander philosophically committed to stemming unnecessary losses, it is quite probable that, given the choice, Pétain would have abandoned the dangerous right-bank positions completely after 25 February.

There is no doubt that the evacuation of this area would have saved the lives of many men as well as valuable war materials. It would also have shortened the overstretched line thereby making the overall French position more tenable. Moreover, the move would have denied the enemy the immediate and continuing chance to sap further the strength of the defending force. Thus, Falkenhayn's strategy would have been scuppered early on. But the option was never available to Pétain. Had he put forward such a suggestion, it would have been considered to constitute nothing less than an unpatriotic act of the highest order, and in all probability, would have seen Pétain replaced by a commander more in keeping with the ideals advocated by Joffre, de Castlenau, et al.

Nevertheless, despite the obvious restrictions, he was able to start lessening the suffering of those troops who had been at Verdun since before the onslaught began. Firstly, he instigated a curtailing of the scale of French counter-attacks on the battlefield, reducing their number until the ratio of possibly successful offensives compared with pointless ones could be raised. Secondly, he obtained his superior's consent for the introduction of a system of troop rotation, known as the *Noria*.

This was Pétain's response to the recognition that soldiers left in the combat zone for too long became physically tired and psychologically demoralized, thereby severely impairing their effective fighting capacities. Under the *Noria* system, divisions would be kept in line for only a short time – tours tended to last from two to eight days – and were relieved before their physical and mental capabilities became too strained. Pétain explained the system as being 'a sort of rotary movement, like that of a millwheel'.

After each visit to the front line – having been 'called on to bear its burden of the bloodshed and weariness on the Verdun front' – each unit was 'returned to the rear or was sent to a quieter sector, there to recover and become again available for other purposes'. It was calculated that fatalities could be more readily replaced in this manner. The instigation of *Noria* meant that more than two-thirds of available French fighting battalions – some 259 out of a total of 330 – served for some length of time at the Battle of Verdun.

The Germans, on the other hand, tended not to rotate their divisions at Verdun and, in the longer term, this gave the French an advantage. German units were kept in line for longer, and losses were simply replaced from behind the line. The German 5th Division, for example, was in line throughout the whole of February, then 8–15 March, and again from 22 April until the end of May. The 25th Division was at the front from 27 February until 16 March, then 10–25 April, and, after a short break, until 19 May. It has been calculated that, between March and the end of May, these two divisions between them lost over 8500 men or, put another way, all of their technical fighting strength. This reality had the effect of gradually wearing out those soldiers engaged at the Battle of Verdun. It also meant that, as the battle went on, the German fighting force became ever more reliant on younger troops with little battle experience to their credit, and, on occasion, inadequate formal military training.

After a while, German intelligence was unable to determine from where the French were getting their men; estimates of dead far outstripped the reality of the numbers on the battlefield. In more practical terms, the ability of the French to replenish human resources and to keep a constant number of troops engaged at Verdun had a definite impact on the German infantry's morale, and this became more pronounced as the battle wore on. The High Command, meanwhile, was tricked into believing that French losses were far higher than they actually were.

The bleak fact, however, is that whatever schemes Pétain or others might have devised as a means of improving the lot of the troops, life was insufferable for the soldiers engaged at Verdun. It was more or less the same on both sides. From almost the moment they arrived, men were subjected to the worst kinds of degradations imaginable until, eventually, they were either maimed, killed, or, for the most fortunate, retired from the front.

The entire experience of the battle was coloured by a number of inescapable factors that, frustratingly, lay beyond the control of the rank and file. The heavy and incessant shelling remained ever present and was more often than not matched in intensity by the infantry fighting. In turn – and there was little respite – this created conditions that ensured that the basic necessities of food, water, and warmth were consistently denied to the combatants. Other determinants, such as the extreme weather conditions, served to compound the misery. Then there was the onset of mental and physical exhaustion and affliction. Almost everyone, regardless of military rank, was affected to some extent by one or other of these disorders. For the wounded at Verdun there was little adequate provision; for the fit, a complete absence of solace.

All that any soldier could hope for was that those in command paid greater attention to the smaller details of operations, such as ensuring that supplies regularly got through to their intended destination. At first, the Germans were better at this. Their line was under far less strain initially, and it constituted a major part of their detailed preplanning. But the length of the campaign, coupled with the pressing demands of it, meant that a high level of commitment to the force's overall well-being could not be maintained. The French, on the other hand, seemed always to be less well prepared. After Pétain's arrival, there was some small improvement in general conditions. But this did not change the fact that life remained intolerably hard for the *poilus* at Verdun.

It was taken largely for granted during the Battle of Verdun that the men would put up with the kind of deprivations that denied basic human necessities and even the smallest of comforts. It was an accepted part of battle life and a great leveller of men. Remarkably, however, there were few instances of disobedience. Every day, human endurance was tested to the limit, and often beyond. But, where conditions allowed, the situation was borne with dignity and an astonishingly ruthless determination that sometimes bordered on nihilism.

The longer-term after-effects of the experience of Verdun remain difficult to quantify. It is true that both mental and physical scars of the battle
were equally deep. Ultimately, however, the non-fatal physical injuries
would heal. The same was not always true of the psychological damage
inflicted at Verdun.

Even the most cursory exploration of the conditions in which men lived
and died at Verdun is utterly depressing. There is nothing that can truly
bring home to one who was not there the barbaric inhumanity suffered by
men, often for weeks at a time, in the course of a campaign involving two
modern, civilized nations. Indescribably traumatic experiences of a most
gruesome nature were a daily fact of life throughout the battle. They form
the backdrop against which this most brutal of battles was fought.

For the German infantry, life at Verdun began in the *Stollen*. These
underground bunkers had been designed only as temporary accommodation, and were not suited to the longer-term occupation caused by the
delayed start to the battle. Compared with the trenches the *poilus* initially
found themselves in, however, the *Stollen* were almost luxurious.

The trenches at Verdun were little different from elsewhere along the
Western Front, nor was life in them. The perennial problems that effected
all trench-dwellers everywhere were the same. The lice and rats, which
lived among the men and their possessions, seemed the only ones to thrive
under such circumstances. There were the insanitary conditions, and
accompanying stench, which fouled absolutely everything. Endless hours
were spent just waiting, not knowing what was going on or when something might happen. There was the ever-present fear of falling victim to a
cunning sniper's bullet or of being buried alive by an exploding shell.
Finally, there were the vagaries of the weather.

At Verdun in 1916, men were left exposed to the elements night and
day sometimes for weeks at a time. During the long winter months there
was the freezing cold; it was always damp; and the putrid mud was usually
ankle deep and caked everything. Nothing escaped ruination under such
conditions – rations, weapons, uniforms – and men were rarely warm.
The only way out was to burrow a small shelter into the trench wall. This
was outlawed in the German and British armies but not in the French.
Consequently, it was common for a *poilu* to spend all his spare time pains-
takingly digging an alcove that would ultimately offer some protection
from the weather and a rare chance to sleep in relative comfort and in the
dry.

But the very nature of the Battle of Verdun dictated that trenches were
little more than temporary features liable at any moment to disappear.
The artillery on both sides would deliberately target opposition trenches,

The hell of Verdun

and as a result, they had constantly to be re-dug. The safest time to undertake this strenuous task was in the hours before dawn, when there would be some let-up in the artillery fire and, if conditions were favourable, the new trench might be waist-deep. But more often than not the effort would be in vain. The following day, perhaps within hours, the new position would be obliterated once again. In truth, then, trenches had little value at Verdun either as a means of shielding men from the enemy or as tenable defensive positions. The German novelist and playwright, Arnold Zweig (1887–1968), noted that trenches were 'impossible to stay in . . . when the very earth quivered and split, and leapt in volcanoes to the sky or poured into ever fresh abysses that were open on every side'.

So the soldiers of both armies, constantly left without any kind of shelter, did the best they could under the circumstances, and took cover wherever and whenever it was possible. Sometimes, this meant taking refuge behind a pile of corpses or a few sodden sandbags. But nothing could effectively stave off the cold and the wet. One German Private wrote home:

> We can't get away from the cold, the rain, the snow, and the mud, and we camp out in the open. Each man digs himself in as best he can, wraps himself up in his coat and canvas bag, and freezes all night. To make matters worse, we are constantly under an artillery fire which claims a large number of victims every evening, for we have no trenches or shelter . . .

Sleep was not easily achieved in the open and amidst an infernal, incessant artillery barrage. The French writer Maurice Genevoix spoke of there being at Verdun, 'A monstrous creature [that] sweeps towards us, so heavy that its flight alone flattens us against the mud'. It was not uncommon for men to go for days on end without proper rest, perhaps for as long as their tour of duty lasted. This fact added another dimension of discomfort to the grisly horrors of the Verdun battlefield.

There are no metaphors that can adequately describe the horror of existence for the soldiers of Verdun. They lived and they died in circumstances so appalling that even the most battle-hardy found them difficult to come to terms with. Always haunted by the spectre of death, the atmosphere created by the elements, the intensity of the fighting, the lack of cover and adequate rest, and more, was surreal. Every moment of the battle witnessed the sudden unfolding of the most harrowing of sights – a comrade ripped to shreds by a shell, or levelled by a bullet, or burned to death by a flame-thrower. Entire rows of men could be seen meeting in an instant the most dreadful of ends. The French artilleryman, Henri Croisilles, recalled seeing an infantryman 'cut in two' when a 305-mm shell landed near where he was standing. 'He pulled himself forward on his hands, in a trail of blood, leaving half of his body behind him, and crying, crying . . .'

This was a typical and expected occurrence, the likes of which had long since lost any sense of terror. Everyone engaged at the Verdun zone accepted that the same could happen to them, at any moment and from any direction. Croisilles observed that:

> The atrocities of a wicked war no longer chill our vigour. An hour later, these bloody visions lose their acuteness, and one goes on with the task one had already begun, with the same obstinate fatalism, but with accentuated bitterness.

In May, he wrote further: 'Death is no longer a mysterious, paralysing, sovereign power – [but] rather a familiar, who wearies us, disgusts us, sends us to sleep'. A French officer, who was a doctor in civilian life, noted laconically from the battlefield that, 'Others live their lives: we begin to live our death . . .'

It was usual to find whole divisions almost annihilated by the enemy onslaught, and fighting in small isolated groups wherever they happened to find themselves on the battlefield. Jacques Meyer recalled how 'commanders of regiments, battalions and even sometimes companies no longer knew where their men were, or the men, where their lines were'. Sometimes, without leadership and cut off from their command headquarters, soldiers would be forced to defend their position without relief, perhaps to a bitter end when the last of their number had fallen. In such instances, troops tended to attack as the best way to ensure that they were not killed. Inflicting damage on the enemy might be the furthest thing from their mind; they simply wished to live to see another day.

Meyer wrote that, in combat at the Battle of Verdun, the best one could hope for was 'to know in the morning where you will be that night'. But there were no guarantees nor, under the circumstances, could there be any. The experience of one French lieutenant is particularly telling:

> I sent out several reconnoitring parties. None of them returned . . . I had no further communication with Headquarters. Ammunition and food had already run short. For my part, I had nothing to eat or drink. Hunger made me unsteady on my feet, and I did not like to ask the men for one of their biscuits. In looking round me a terrifying idea took hold of me: – we were separated from the living. A door had shut down brutally on our existence, on our past, and we were precipitated into a vast, black night.

Thus was the sense of desolation experienced absolute. This was indeed an existence like no other, a parallel world of stunning brutality and deprivation, for which no previous experiences could have prepared the soldiers of Verdun.

Often, the only link between this and the outside world was via a runner. The task was a thankless one – as unrewarding as being a member of a rations party – and imbued with great dangers. The mortality rate among runners was exceptionally high but there was never any shortage of volunteers on the French side for, as Georges Blond has explained, the job

> accorded with the French soldier's high degree of individuality, his desire to be singled out for his intelligence, to function outside the limits of

everyday discipline, and in some ways to share the secrets of his superiors. In return he was ready to use his wits and to outdo himself in daring.

It is a measure of how poor military practices were at the time of World War I that, once lines of communication were cut, commanders had no alternative but to deploy humans to relay orders, knowing full well that there was only the slightest chance that the command would reach its intended destination. Nevertheless, there were occasional instances of great heroism. A French bugler of the 33rd Regiment, called Haverland, was reported to have shuttled between his major and a colonel for some ninety-six hours without rest, covering over and again 1500 metres or so 'of shell-swept ground to carry messages'.

On a battlefield where cover was at a premium, men would often take up shelter in craters created by the impact of heavy calibre artillery shells. This was a precarious practice but it did tend to offer mild respite from the intense bombardment raging overhead. It was common for these holes to be shared with rotting corpses. A French Captain, Gillet, remembered craters 'in which corpses float like flies in a basin'. Sometimes a wounded man would be visible lying among the dead, having been left for hours or perhaps days. Generally, even if they were close by, those who laid injured on the battlefield would not be offered assistance by an able-bodied colleague for the slightest movement made them a target for enemy machine-gunners. So, unless soldiers were sure they were safe, the fallen were left untended. This added another grim dimension to the scene, as one eyewitness recalled: 'Every evening . . . one hears the cries of agony, the delirious ravings of the wounded whom one cannot relieve because of the violence of the fusillade and the bombardment'.

For the same reasons, the dead could not be readily collected for burial. Falling shells and gunfire made the battle zone a place that was not ventured across unless absolutely necessary. Consequently, the dead were left to decompose where they had fallen. When circumstances allowed, the only solution to this problem was to wrap a number of corpses together in a large canvas sheet and roll this into a big shell hole. This was only partly effective. A new shell would inevitably disinter the package and blow the bodies into ever-smaller pieces. As a result, the battle area was littered with unidentifiable torsos, limbs, and other body parts that would hang or lie wherever they had been blown. The dead and human parts were scattered everywhere.

But the men of Verdun soon became immune to the horrors that were all about them. A dull fear stayed with most soldiers, however: unsurprising, in that a life could be taken, without warning, at any moment. But the sheer terror that, at first, would freeze them to the spot, soon passed. In

The infantry engaged at Verdun soon became immune to the attendant horrors of the battle. Here, French troops play a game of cards

the end, men got used to living with and among the dead and the dying. Indeed, it was considered the norm, as a kind of psychosis quickly enveloped all those in the grips of the so-called 'death ravines of Verdun'. It followed, therefore, that, after a day or two at Verdun, no one so much as blinked at the carnage that lay around them like so much litter: the human corpses, rotting and at various stages of decomposition; the hunks of mud-stained and bloody flesh; the severed limbs protruding from the earth; the pools of vomit and mounds of human and animal excrement; the fallen horses, dead but with a crazed expression still discernible; upturned and burning vehicles; the cold metal of expended shell cases; tree stumps, the only visible remains of what had once been dense woodlands; and everywhere the sickly sweet smell of death, the ghastly stink of putrefaction which, according to one soldier, was 'so disgusting that it almost gives a certain charm to the odour of gas shells'.

When it rained, the battle zone – which, after a few weeks of fighting, resembled a mass shallow grave – would be turned into a swamp. 'The mud', one combatant noted, 'can be as fatal as bullets.' Men would sink into this churning mass, often drowning in a stinking quagmire that resembled quicksand in its consistency. Then, in the summer months, when the stench that hovered over the battlefield worsened and the earth baked over, the threat of the mud subsided only to be replaced by another.

Thirst claimed a steady harvest of fatalities from both sides. Water was often simply not available to men who found themselves isolated and cut

Wounded French troops, from the Verdun front

off from even the most tenuous of supply lines. Under these conditions, soldiers would suffer for days on end, increasingly ravaged by a dryness that guaranteed a slow death. Out of sheer desperation, some drank from the stagnant water at the bottom of shell craters or tried to drink their own urine. Where water was available, it was not always safe to drink because chlorine from gas shells or disease from disinterred bodies had polluted it. Many men were poisoned in this way, killed not by the enemy's weaponry but by their own basic needs. This truly highlights the desperate conditions under which the Battle of Verdun was waged.

Yet avoidable fatalities marred this and every other battle fought along the Western Front during World War I. It is true that the weapons employed at Verdun accounted for most of the dead. Unlike bullets, heavy calibre guns were undiscerning and could kill dozens at a time. Gas, too, had an enormous effect and was a particularly nasty way to die, usually with fits and convulsions, if the noxious fumes did not take immediate effect. But many thousands of others died at Verdun simply because the mechanisms for saving and treating them were either not operating effectively or did not exist at all. For the French, especially, if wounded in action, the chances of survival were poor. At the war's end, from a total of 1.3 million dead, France had lost some 400,000 men from the effects of wounds; by far the highest proportion of fatalities suffered in this way by any of the main protagonists. This was because French medical provision was inadequate and based, as Lyn Macdonald has observed, 'on the

requirements of a swift war of manoeuvre and . . . [not] the actual circumstances that had now prevailed for over a year'. Thus, doctors were forced
to act according to so-called 'conservation of effectives'. This dictated that
attention was given primarily to those who could be healed and returned
to the battle front. If those who could not be saved could not be moved
elsewhere, they were just left to die, often in great misery and pain,
because scant resources would not be spent on easing their condition.
Others who could be saved but would clearly be of no further military
use, would be attended only if materials and circumstances allowed. At
the busiest medical centres, more often than not such cases would not be
treated.

It was, however, an achievement for a wounded French soldier to make
it to a hospital or medical clearing station at all. There were not enough
stretcher-bearers and, across much of the battle area, they simply could
not get through the bombardment to collect the injured. Even if a
wounded soldier was picked up, the chances of him getting back from the
front alive were slim. First, the enemy's fire had to be avoided. Then there
were the ambulances. These were slow-moving, often converted vehicles
with the thinnest of hardened tyres on which to drive over poorly serviced and pot-holed roads. For those hanging on to life by a thread, such a
journey usually posed a most serious threat.

Even when these problems were surmounted, there was only a one in
three chance of an injured Frenchman leaving hospital alive. Medical
posts operated under great stress and tended to be in continual disarray.
The atmosphere of these places did little to revive flagging spirits nor did it
give much cause for optimism. The sights and sounds that greeted a new
arrival were usually ghastly. Blond described the 'horrors of the first-aid
post' thus:

> the men holding their intestines in both hands, the broken bones tearing
> the flesh, the arteries spurting blood as a clot gave way, bared brains . . . the
> maimed hand ("What were you in civilian life?" "A sculptor."), the empty
> eye sockets, the pierced chests, the skin hanging down in tatters from the
> burned face, the missing lower jaw . . .

A volunteer ambulance driver of the American Field Service, Henry
Sheahan, described the scene at a converted château hospital, a few kilometres outside the city of Verdun:

> The Château reeked of ether and idoform. Pasty-faced, tired attendants
> unloaded mud, cloth, bandages and blood that turned out to be human be-
> ings; an overwrought doctor-in-chief screamed contradictory orders at

everybody, and flared into cries of hysterical rage. Ambulance after ambulance came from the lines full of clients; kindly hands pulled out the stretchers, and bore them to the washroom . . . The wounded lay [there] naked in their stretchers while the attendant daubed them with a hot soapy sponge – the blood ran from their wounds through the stretchers to the floor, and seeped into the cracks of the stones.

Other medical stations were neither as well staffed nor as efficient as the one described. At some, there was a shortage of 'kindly hands' and even exhausted, over-worked auxiliaries. It was not uncommon for there to be a lack of beds and available shelter, and for new cases simply to be unloaded from the ambulance and left in the open, perhaps on a lawn or stretch of road. Rats had to be beaten from the prostrated with sticks. If there was a backlog of casualties – as was usual at most medical stations at the height of the battle – men would simply expire before receiving even the most rudimentary treatment.

This reflected the fact that the French medical services, inadequate as they were, also suffered from extremely poor organization. There was a shortage of absolutely everything, from surgeons and doctors to ambulances and vital drugs, such as antiseptics, and other necessities such as bandages. There were no adequate sedatives in 1916, and morphine was administered to a patient only when he had reached the operating table. Furthermore, the general lack of human resources meant that there was an unhealthy reliance on volunteers – mostly from the United States and Britain – to fill vital roles such as driving ambulances and nursing the sick.

Hospitals were usually improvized affairs because the German artillery had wrecked those hastily established in the Verdun zone before the battle. Because there were not enough doctors, those called to duty at Verdun worked intolerably long hours usually in the most squalid and insanitary conditions. It was not uncommon for them to have to operate by candlelight, with their hands covered in blood, mud, and filth. At the Château d'Esnes, on the left bank of the Meuse, two doctors worked around the clock, operating for 24 hours a day, assisted only by a chaplain. It was a similar story at another château hospital, some 40 kilometres from Verdun at Rivigny.

To try to stem the flow of casualties coming from the front field surgeons were more frequently called in. Yet, soon, they, too, were engulfed in the same madness as their colleagues behind the line, working with inadequate equipment and under imperfect conditions. Mostly, field surgeons had no access to anaesthetics and were forced to work without them, performing amputations and the like without any medically recognized painkillers. Such operations usually resulted in death.

The hospital dead would be piled high – according to one witness 'like things devoid of use'. The human and material waste of the first-aid posts would intermingle while all about the loathsome stench of death filled the air. The only sounds able to compete with the crashing shells were the screams of the wounded, crying out in anguish from their suffering. The horror was indiscriminate and, as the battle wore on, the German line – so well prepared for a strictly limited number of casualties – found itself increasingly beset by the same problems of evacuating and treating the injured and burying of the dead.

For ten months Verdun was a furnace from which came every manner of suffering and dying imaginable. The unrelenting intensity of the warfare seen there in 1916, coupled with the length of the battle, guaranteed that, even by World War I standards, it was a horrendous experience. Little that happened at Verdun was unique to that part of the Western Front but, arguably, it was only here that the accompanying horrors were so extreme and persisted for so long.

Those who survived Verdun were never the same again. It was not only the physical suffering that betrayed the full terror of the ordeal. Among the French, it was reputedly discernible in their stare. Some, of course, remained outwardly unaffected by their time at Verdun. But the glazed expression was nearly always evident. The most unfortunate were driven mad by what they had been through but even the most stoic could not remain completely immune to the pitiless hand fate had dealt them. By the late spring, Verdun's reputation had spread beyond the ranks of those who had served there to the rest of the French Army. Fresh relieving forces arriving at the sector were urged by their retreating comrades not to go any further. But they always did.

As the battle developed and took a turn that Falkenhayn had never intended, the Germans suffered just the same. Werner Beumelberg wrote in his history of Verdun, that the conflict:

> transformed men's souls. Whoever floundered through this morass full of the shrieking and the dying, whoever shivered in those nights, had passed the last frontier of life, and henceforth bore deep within him the leaden memory of a place that lies between Life and Death, or perhaps beyond either . . .

The very awfulness of the battle poses the question: why did the men at Verdun follow orders almost to the letter when to do so meant being knowingly subjected to the worst kind of physical and mental barbarity imaginable?

In his history of the Battle of Verdun, Alistair Horne suggests that, by 1916, the soldiers of World War I had ceased to be concerned by questions of ideology – or by related issues such as nationalism – but rather, they fought from 'a tough kind of cynicism'. He writes that:

[the soldier of 1916] no longer considered himself fighting for such noble symbols as Alsace, Belgium, the Vaterland or rule of the seas. He fought simply out of a helpless sense of habit, to keep going, to keep alive . . . [I]t seemed as if the man at the front could continue to accept almost indefinitely. Physically and morally, both the French and the Germans had become toughened to the act of acceptance; as it were, inoculated against the afflictions of war.

This seems to have been the rule, at least among infantrymen, and only a few reservations were expressed by officers or artillerymen (Croisilles, for example, explained that in his view, 'Were the end not great and noble, we should not serve it thus unquestioningly'). Some German soldiers appear after a while to have been fighting for anything other than the glory and prestige of their nation. Dominik Richert, an Alsatian enlisted in the German Army and possibly fighting a war in which he wished to see 'his' side defeated, observed that 'In truth, courage has nothing to do with it. The fear of death surpasses all other feelings and terrible compulsion alone drives the soldier forward'. A Grenadier, Rudolf Koch, explained:

We never understood the sense of the entire operation . . . The soldier does his duty and does not question why. It was duty alone that kept us together and held our courage up. At such a place, one cannot speak of enthusiasm; everyone wishes they were a thousand miles away . . .

Richert concurs with this last point, stating 'not a man would have remained voluntarily at the front'.

The well-known dramatist, Ernst Toller, who had volunteered his services to the German military at the outbreak of the war, retold his progression through the whole gamut of emotions from unabashed ideologue to the realization that he was but a small cog in his country's vast and unrelenting war effort:

The great patriotic feelings turn dull, the big words small; war becomes commonplace, service at the front day's work; heroes become victims, volunteers slaves; life is one hell, death a mere trifle; we are all screws in a machine that wallows forward, nobody knows where to.

So men accepted the horrific task they had been sent to do, albeit with a certain air of bitterness and cynicism. Most memoirs concerning Verdun betray a sense that, in most people's experience, there was no feasible escape from the inferno other than through death. Consequently, a perceptible fatalism took hold of the majority of those fighting on both sides at Verdun. In turn, as the battle dragged on, compassion across the line became more commonplace. One came to know the mind of one's enemy, to understand that he was experiencing much the same emotional and psychological cycles. When circumstances allowed, as opposing positions became more compressed and there was a lull in the fighting, such sentiment might be articulated, with one set of soldiers commiserating with the other about the terrible wickedness of the war. As in so many other gruesome battles, the average foot-soldier, commanded to carry out orders, became increasingly aware with time that the real enemy might not necessarily be the man in the trench opposite. One German private even pleaded from the front at Verdun: 'If only this wretched war would end! No one who has any sense can justify such a butchery of men.'

The common, though unstated, bond between the two infantries on the ground was perhaps reinforced by the sense that they understood better than most what it truly meant to be involved at the Battle of Verdun. Certainly, those who had not experienced the battle could not begin to comprehend the atrocities being perpetrated there.

This made time on leave away from the battle zone particularly difficult for most. Throughout France, the best efforts of the official censor guaranteed that the full scale of the horrors and sufferings of the battle never reached the population at large, and that only a sanitized – or positive – version of events at Verdun ever reached the public. Thus were French losses always 'negligible', defences 'heroic', and gains – however slight they might actually have been – portrayed as being of epic and noble proportions. It was little wonder, then, that, on rare excursions from the battle area, the French soldiers of Verdun were baffled by the widely held notions they came across. Most unnerving was the fact that no one seemed fully to understand what they had been put through.

The *poilus* rarely enjoyed their time on leave, and tended to spend it behind the line eating, sleeping, and trying to escape from the incessant crashing of shells. On their pitiful pay of five sous (or one-twentieth of a franc) a day, few could afford to go home. Nor, away from the front, were there any clubs for them to frequent or canteens offering cheap food and wine. Further, the sights and sounds of life behind the line would, more often than not, sicken them. Life in many a French town remained relatively 'good' throughout the war. Yet such a 'normal' atmosphere would make the average *poilu* feel ill at ease. Many would return to the line ahead of time, to what they knew and were used to, and to their friends. Here, in their own version of normality, they were understood and, conversely, could comprehend what was expected of them. It was a sad and deprived life that offered no chance of real respite from the war. Such was the lot of the Frenchmen at the Battle of Verdun.

6

Resistance

ils ne passeront pas
(they shall not pass)

DESPITE HIS 60 years of age, Pétain had lost none of his stature, and remained an imposing figure who gave off certain air of assuredness to those who came into contact with him. There were indeed some who were not in the least surprised by his elevation through the ranks of the French Army during World War I. For, though Pétain consistently made enemies from his equals and superiors and continually proclaimed ideas that were anathema to those who mattered most, others who had served under him tended to have nothing but admiration for the man and for his working methods.

One of his foremost protégées, who saw action at Verdun and was taken prisoner in late February 1916 near the village of Douaumont, was the young Charles de Gaulle. So impressed had he been by Pétain's instructions at the War College that, upon graduating, he applied to serve under his command. He had the utmost regard for Pétain's personal rectitude, noting that 'His independence and integrity, while allowing him to take orders and receive advice, made him immune from influence'. He further approved of Pétain's abilities as a commander, writing that he 'taught his army to distinguish the real from the imaginary and the possible from the impossible'.

These strengths of character were no secret and, had he not possessed them, the French General Staff would not have been convinced that Pétain was the right man for the job of trying to save Verdun. In this respect, his reputation as a natural leader preceded him and, though the French Army's hierarchy may not have trusted Pétain's beliefs, they had implicit confidence in his ability to face up to this most serious of undertakings with a steady resolve.

It was also recognized that, if anyone could bolster sagging morale throughout the line at Verdun, it was Pétain. He was highly regarded among the *poilus* who tended to view him as a rather paternal figure. There existed here a relationship of mutual respect and great trust. Pétain

LA GRANDE GUERRE 1914-15 16   Visé Bourges 432
VERDUN-sur-MEUSE 1916 - Habitations en Ruines

Verdun houses after an artillery attack

was seen as someone who cared for the general well-being of the soldiers and who might try to improve their lot while, simultaneously, striving to conserve their numbers. Further, the rank-and-file believed that, if Pétain gave an order, then there must be some reason for it. He was distinguished from those vainglorious generals who, for the sake of vanity and fleeting prestige, would sacrifice hundreds or thousands of lives if it meant gaining a few metres of ultimately profitless ground from the enemy.

Before the ignominy of his surrender to the Nazis in 1940, Pétain enjoyed great popular fame throughout France. During this time, survivors of Verdun were prepared to admit openly that Pétain was no butcher of men and would applaud his almost unique sensitivity to the *poilu*'s 'individual existence': he refused to regard them as a characterless mass of charnel-house fodder. His influence over the soldiers and the high regard in which they held him were compounded by his seeming instinct for saying and doing the right thing at the right time. On a visit to the front, for example, he would always inquire after the injured, and apportion blame and praise in the correct proportions and to the right persons.

He was further respected for his steady nerve and outward calm. The French politician, Paul Painlevé, recalled of Pétain during the crisis days at Verdun, his 'impassive face, his gaze that nothing troubled in the gravest of circumstances; his organiser's brain that only left the inevitable to chance'. This might have been little more than a façade, for later at Verdun Pétain was to suffer from a worsening tic of the eye that betrayed inner turmoil and a deepening sense of foreboding. Nevertheless, his presence managed to inspire confidence throughout French ranks during the darkest days of the battle.

Pétain was always thought to be more of a tactician than a strategist and, on arriving at the battle zone, tactics would be his most pressing concern. But first he had to invoke some of the popular mystique that had become attached to his name, and act in a manner that could engender some sense of belief. General de Castlenau's affirmative actions had certainly stopped the rot but the fall of Fort Douaumont was to shake confidence seriously, and a general sense of panic still lingered. Even at General Herr's headquarters, no one really believed de Castlenau when he stated that Verdun could be saved, and most expected the sector eventually to fall, perhaps sooner rather than later. Only Joffre it seemed, at the safe distance of his command post at Chantilly, and his representative on the spot, de Castlenau, were not totally imbued with an acute sense of pessimism.

The scenes that Pétain saw as he approached Verdun were indicative of the calamitous situation the French now found themselves in. There was disorder was everywhere. Vehicles could progress along the road only at a slow walking pace and with some luck. All routes were continuously blocked by a seething mass of confused humanity scurrying in all directions yet ultimately going nowhere. The icy and muddy conditions served merely to hinder all routes out of the turmoil. At a standstill along the road, there were ambulances carrying patients, horses dragging field guns, army cars transporting commanders, trucks moving supplies. On the soft verges and among the stationary traffic, a steady flow of civilian refugees straggled away from the city, taking all the possessions they could carry. Among this stream could be seen the flotsam of shattered and shell-shocked units, retreating defeated from the front, dirty and exhausted with heads lowered. Reinforcing troops tried to push against this tide but in no discernible order and with only partial success. Horses skated about on the precariously icy surface; trucks were upended and left abandoned in ditches. Under such circumstances, how could Verdun be saved? Without fresh troops and vital supplies, the cause was lost. Yet nothing was getting through the chaos and up to the line.

Pétain was deeply moved by what he saw and, reportedly, had to hold back the tears. Yet, on reaching Verdun, matters were worse still. The situation was indeed a desperate one. When Pétain asked, no one on General Herr's staff could pin-point the positions of the Corps on the battlefield. There were no maps of troops' positions, no records of infantry deployments, no log of recent commands given. In fact, no one could adequately summarize what orders, if any, had been passed down the line in the last few hours. Herr himself was clearly on the verge of a complete breakdown while some were calling for his head as a scapegoat.

Pétain had seen enough. He retreated to Souilly, a village off the main road linking Verdun with Bar-le-Duc, and set up headquarters, hoping that he might find there 'a little more calm'. His immediate goal was to instil some order into French operations at Verdun, and give them greater direction by mustering increasing efficiency out of the confusion. In the short term, the best he could do was to make use of the human and material resources available to him methodically and with improved effectiveness.

The new command took control at Verdun at the stroke of midnight on 25–6 February. Pétain immediately contacted General Balfourier and informed him: 'I have taken over command. Tell your troops. Hold fast. I have confidence in you.' Then he acted swiftly, in a manner most likely to allow the battered French forces indeed to 'hold fast' against the vastly superior enemy. He divided the general battle zone into four smaller, more manageable sectors, and put a trusted general in command of each. Thus, General Duchesne and his charges were directed towards the Meuse heights; General Bezelaire was to remain on the left bank, overseeing operations from Avocourt, east to the boundary created by the River Meuse; on the right bank, General Guillamat's command would secure the area from the Meuse to Douaumont; and east of Douaumont, Balfourier's troops would hold the line.

Shattered at the end of an eventful few days, Pétain's last act of the day, before retiring for the night, was to sketch out on a map a thick charcoal line indicating the front to be held at all costs by the defending forces. He handed this to his personal Chief of Staff, Colonel de Barescut, then fell asleep in an armchair. No bed could be found at Souilly for the new commander of the French forces at Verdun.

When he awoke the next morning Pétain had a severe fever. The exertions of the past 24 hours, coupled with the freezing cold of night, had caught up with the General, and he would be ill for most of the next week. It was perhaps a common consequence of the rigours Pétain had been put through but one, nonetheless, that the French could hardly afford at this juncture. He refused to succumb to the illness, however, and a cordon of secrecy meant that he was able to direct operations from his sick bed completely unhindered.

Despite his illness, he was immediately able to pull some semblance of order from the chaos that was destabilizing the French line. He quickly concluded that, from a tactical point of view, the general situation was not so bad as it had first appeared. He later recalled that:

> Considering the terrific force of the enemy's drive, the fact that Verdun was still in our possession on February 25th constituted really a success.

The loss of our advanced positions to a depth of five or six kilometres represented nothing more serious than a normal setback, one which we might have contemplated without anxiety in regard to its results.

Furthermore, he was assured by the facts that reinforcements – Balfourier's XX Corps – had already reached Verdun and that an additional two corps were on their way up the line, with more promised. If the French could hold out for at least another 48 hours, Pétain predicted, the general decline could be reversed and Verdun saved.

In the meantime, it was imperative that no further costly mistakes were committed, that the French inflicted upon themselves no other needless wounds. Pétain realized that if there were to be a repeat of the catastrophes at Samogneux or Fort Douaumont, the already strained defence was liable to crack completely. He set about ensuring that there would be none. His first Order of the Day was to the point, simply instructing what everyone already knew: 'to check at all costs the attacks of the enemy; to retake at once all lost ground'. France could ill afford to be pushed back any further. Nevertheless, he curtailed the counter-moves designed to recapture some of the ground *already* lost and, to this end, revoked de Castlenau's order to retake Fort Douaumont immediately. One hastily arranged attempt had already failed dismally and, under the circumstances, Pétain was all too aware that any others were likely to end in heavy French losses. 'Conserve your strength' became the new guiding mantra.

A tactical realignment of the French defensive lines, based on the most readily tenable positions, was then instigated. This was the so-called 'Line of Resistance' that ran from Souville, north to Thiaumont, tightly around the position of Fort Douaumont to Vaux, down to Moulainville, and then in a line along the ridge of the Woërve Plain. According to Pétain, this represented 'a position marked on the right bank by the very lines that we were holding at the moment and that left us no free ground for any possible further retirement'.' A similar line was instigated on the left bank, through Cumières, the Mort Homme, Côte 304, and Avocourt.

The backbone of the 'Line of Resistance' was to consist of the system of fortresses that had been so sadly neglected up until this point. Each was to be bulwarked through rearmament and the designation of its own commander and a fresh, numerically adequate garrison with two weeks' worth of full supplies. These would follow strict orders, designed to ensure 'that no earthwork should be evacuated or surrendered even in case it were completely surrounded and cut off'. It was hoped that, in this way, there could be no repeat of the débâcle that had seen Fort Douaumont fall so easily.

Finally, a confidential 'Line of Panic' was also drawn up. This would become operative only in the event of the 'Line of Resistance' folding and the French being forced to undertake a last, desperate defence of the city of Verdun. The line ran, almost straight, to the north of Verdun through the forts of Belleville, St Michel, and Moulainville.

The new command now turned its attention to the vexing problem of communications. As Pétain had already seen for himself, until a feasible, fully operational link was established between the Verdun sector and the rest of France, all would be lost. As matters stood, Verdun could be serviced only in a most tenuous and unsustaining manner. The main rail line had been severed by the enemy, and a secondary one was under constant artillery bombardment. This left only an inadequate narrow-gauge railway, known as the *Musien* – which could not be expected properly to service the current requirements of the Verdun sector – and the second-class road that ran between Verdun and Bar-le-Duc. It was on the latter that Pétain chose to concentrate, deciding that this must be employed to its maximum capacity if it were to serve as a viable lifeline for the front at Verdun.

The road was some 55 kilometres long, and quickly became integral to all French operations at Verdun. Absolutely everything that was required to sustain the French defence there – from bandages and tins of grease to artillery pieces, horses, and infantry corps – poured along this winding path. It is estimated that some half-a-million men (a weekly average of 90,000), 17,000 animals, and 11,000 trucks a week used the road, forming an endless convoy night and day. Because of its importance, this route became enshrined throughout France as the *Voie Sacrée* or 'Sacred Way'.

Traffic was kept flowing by the enforcement of a strict set of rules drawn up by Pétain – and the engineer responsible for the overall running of the road, Major Richard – and put into practice immediately. Only motor vehicles – most of which had been requisitioned by the army for the war effort – were permitted to use the road; all troops and other pedestrians needing access were to march beside it. The road was to be employed for military purposes only. No unauthorized use of the way was allowed. Furthermore, there was a strict order of priorities dictating exactly what or who passed along the way: ammunition, guns, and soldiers first; everything else – including ambulances – second. This rule was closely observed. Any breakdowns were to be heaved off of the road immediately so as not to hinder the smooth flow of traffic. Such cases would then be dealt with by a crew of engineers. There was one crew for each of the six sectors that the road had been split into for administrative purposes.

At the height of the activity along the *Voie Sacrée*, during the summer months of 1916, it is estimated that, on average, a vehicle passed along

Voie Sacrée

On taking command at Verdun on 26 February 1916, General Pétain was faced with a number of vexing problems. Undoubtedly, one of the most pressing tasks before him was to ensure the smooth flow of men, munitions, and material up to the battle zone. Until this time, a prevailing chaos had meant that very few vital supplies were getting through to their intended destinations. Pétain was quick to realize that, unless drastic action was taken, the defence of Verdun was a lost cause.

His scope for action in this matter was, however, limited. The main rail link into Verdun had been hit by the German artillery, and a secondary line was under constant bombardment. There was a narrow-gauge railway – the *Musien* – running into the city but, under the circumstances, it could hardly be expected to sustain the many requirements of the Verdun force. This left only the second-class road that ran from Bar-le-Duc to Verdun. From late February, the road was employed to its maximum capacity, becoming Verdun's sole link with the rest of France. As such, it was a central feature of the entire battle, with a significance that should not be underestimated.

Every item required for the French effort at Verdun made its way along this path. It is estimated that an average of 90,000 men, 17,000 animals, and 11,000 trucks carrying 500,000 tonnes of materials used the road every week. By the summer, a vehicle passed along the way on average once every fourteen seconds and, by the battle's end, more than two-thirds of France's infantry had journeyed along the route. The stream of traffic was constant and ran by day and by night. A strict set of rules was enforced to ensure that the flow of vehicles remained uninterrupted and that the road was used for military purposes only. Furthermore, it was determined that troops requiring access to Verdun would not be permitted on to the road itself but would have to march alongside it, and that any breakdowns should be removed immediately so as not to cause any unnecessary delay.

For administrative purposes, the road was divided into six sectors, and each sector was allotted a team of engineers who would deal with any problem vehicles. Gravel and metal were constantly shovelled on to the surface of the road to prevent it from falling into disrepair, and reservists filled in pot-holes and cracks with soft stone quarried from nearby pits.

The effort was a monumental one requiring round-the-clock management. It is undeniable that, without it, the continued defence of the Verdun sector could not have been sustained. The road became quickly enshrined throughout France as the *Voie Sacrée* – the 'sacred way'.

it once every fourteen seconds. Nothing stopped the stream of *materiel* into Verdun. Gravel and metal were both used to bolster the road which held up remarkably well save for a few scares, such as when it turned into a veritable quagmire after a sudden thaw at the end of February. That the road continued to operate at all was because it was being continually repaired (as one observer has noted, the *Voie Sacrée* was forever being deconstructed and reconstructed). Potholes would be filled in by reservists who shovelled soft stone which had been quarried from specially reopened pits nearby. Over the length of the battle, 8000 men continually laid tonnes of stone across the surface of the road. It was some effort.

The impact of the reorganization of the main Bar-le-Duc to Verdun

Memorials to the *Voie Sacrée* (pictured) have been placed at kilometre intervals along the main Bar-le-Duc to Verdun road

road should not be underestimated. Without it, any feasible defence of the Verdun sector would not have been possible. While other initiatives, such as the construction of thirty-six new bridges across the River Meuse, had some effect in allowing the movement of men and materials up to the front, it was primarily via the *Voie Sacrée* that such crucial undertakings were facilitated. The logistics involved were phenomenal

Supplies being brought to the Verdun front

French troops smile for the camera as they move up the line to the battle zone

but, by the same token and as the subsequent course of events was to prove, absolutely necessary.

Pétain's first Order of the Day – requiring the immediate containment of the enemy and the reconquest of lost land – was a tall order for a force that had been continually attacked for days, understrength, and in a state of turmoil. But, because it was Pétain who had given the order, it seemed to take some of the edge off it. Indeed, as the news of his arrival to command operations at Verdun filtered through, the *poilus* took heart. Their waning confidence received a slight, yet much needed, boost.

The General, however, was realistic enough to understand that his ground force was so physically and mentally disoriented that the most that could be asked of it was that it just stood its ground. Consequently, efforts were concentrated on speedily co-ordinating the actions of the artillery. So far, the French artillery had performed only fitfully but Pétain realized that this was not because of its lack of potential but, rather, a lack of direction and order in its actions. It did not require great and immediate effort to improve its performance. Pétain took a direct role in overseeing that artillery operations focused on causing the Germans maximum losses for the least cost to the French. In no time at all, and for the first time since the start of the battle, the French heavy guns began to match those of the enemy, acting in calculated concert. The impact was quickly felt across the German line. Artillery and infantry positions alike were hit, either disabled or knocked out completely, and plans to re-instigate the general advance on Verdun were effectively, if only temporarily, curtailed.

The French were still in no position to make capital out of these successes, however, and, as a result, their impact remained fragmentary and of only limited importance to the overall balance of power across the battlefield. Before matters could be tangibly restored in favour of the French, a huge effort would have to be made in every area of operations. Pétain knew that, to turn the situation around, 'Every man's will must be bent to the task before him, without a glance backward'.

In the week following the fall of Fort Douaumont, fighting on the right bank centred around the village of Douaumont which was situated slightly to the north-west of the fort itself. The infantry combat was at close quarters and particularly ferocious. Both sides had had some chance to replenish the line and remained as committed as ever to ceding not a centimetre of ground. The Germans, of course, could exploit their advantage of having taken Fort Douaumont and, in this vicinity, their infantry could manoeuvre under the protection of shielding machine-gun fire. Nevertheless, the village changed hands on a number of occasions. Losses were high on both sides, with entire battalions being wiped out.

Ultimately, the effect of heavy, long-range, 420-mm shells saw off the French; the Germans were left in control of an area of land that had previously been the site of a thriving village community.

Despite the defeat, the fiery French defence of Douaumont instituted a change in the nature of the battle. The defending forces' fortunes had taken a slight general turn for the better, in small part thanks to the immediate consequences of Pétain's tactical realignment of the French line. Thereafter, the chances of the attacking force being able to achieve the same sort of gains as those made on 24–5 February diminished considerably. The opportunity for achieving an early victory at Verdun passed, and most historians agree that this point marked the passing of the first stage of the Battle of Verdun.

The tempo of the conflict now began to abate. The day of 27 February represented the first time in the campaign when the Germans made no noticeable gains anywhere. This was undoubtedly the result of the new resolve that was evident throughout the French line. But the Germans also had problems of their own. As a thaw set in, the front became swamp-like and the heavier artillery batteries became bogged down in the quagmire. Some artillery pieces were beginning to show signs of wear. Lines of communications also suffered because of the weather. Furthermore, the attacking infantry had, for the first time, hit a blocking wall and this was not without consequence. The Crown Prince noted that, by the end of February, 'the exalted offensive spirit of our troops had been sapped by the physical and moral exhaustion resulting from the excessive strain of the fighting and difficulties of weather and ground'.

These were ominous signs. In a matter of a few days, the impetus that had driven the attacking forces forward, spurred on by a large element of surprise, high spirits, and some tangible early successes, had begun to dissipate. Though, unquestionably, they still held the strategic and tactical advantage, as well as a slight psychological edge, the command of the Fifth Army was all too aware that, on the boggy Meuse battleground, this could be easily frittered away if the French were allowed further respite and the chance to regroup. Already losses were unexpectedly high; 500 men had been lost in one day's fighting for Douaumont village. At home, politicians in the Reichstag were warning against allowing the offensive at Verdun to develop into another Ypres.

By the same token, the new French command had managed admirably to stabilize the defending line, and the dividends of this – largely psychological – were beginning to be felt. The turn about was such that, by the end of February, de Castlenau could predict, with only a little bravado, that 'Verdun was for the moment safe'. He could make this statement

Abri du Kronprinz dans le bois de la Grurie.
Crownprince's shelter in the Grurie wood.

A shelter used by the Crown Prince during operations at Verdun

because the French military machine at Verdun had finally begun to function. Between 27 February and 6 March, some 25,000 tons of ammunition and equipment, 480 artillery guns, and 190,000 men had travelled along the *Voie Sacrée* to the Verdun sector. The front had been adequately reinforced, at least for the time being.

On the battlefield, Pétain's main concern for the moment lay not with the performance of his forces but, rather, with what the Germans would do next. It was calculated that they might try another approach and extend the front of the attack to include the left bank of the Meuse ahead of Verdun. Not only would this further stretch the defending force at a time when they could hardly afford to be stretched but it would also serve to free up the Germans concentrated, and increasingly muddled, line. It would also put pressure on French artillery positions there and jeopardize the free reign they had enjoyed over the past few days. The most effective way, Pétain thought, for French heavy guns to inflict damage upon the enemy was to set them firing from flanking positions on the left bank in a north-easterly direction towards the point of the advancing German infantry line. The assessment had been correct and havoc was being wrought across the German attacking front. The infantry's movements had been arrested, the artillery had stopped functioning so well, and supply lines – providing vital reinforcements of men and materials – were rendered less effective.

All the while, the human slaughter continued. French losses remained constant though the effect was less keenly felt as a result of better communications to the front. The German artillery was exacting a lesser toll, however, at the very moment the French high-calibre guns began to perform. Consequently, German losses were beginning to run at an exceptionally high and unsustainable level. French 75- and 155-mm guns were sweeping all that lay before them and, on the ground, machine-gunners, riflemen, and grenadiers were all achieving notable successes. In one day alone, von Zwehl's VII Reserve Corps – so sprightly throughout the initial stages of the battle – was blitzed by artillery fire and mopped up by the French infantry.

The German Army had begun to suffer in a similar manner to the French. Unless something was done, Falkenhayn's plan was liable to backfire. The secondary goal, of capturing Verdun (just a push away a few days earlier), also started to look less realizable. Still, confidence was high within the Fifth Army's command. On 28 February, the Crown Prince commented that the likelihood of a 'considerable moral and material victory' for Germany at Verdun remained very good.

Others were not quite so sure. The Kaiser aired the belief that, 'This war will end at Verdun'. Falkenhayn, meanwhile, concerned himself with the broadest of strategic pictures and, possibly with an eye to his maxim that the Battle of Verdun should not expend his country's fighting forces unnecessarily, refused the Crown Prince's request, lodged in the last week of February, for reinforcements. Two divisions were blocked at Metz but would be released in due course. Other divisions, meanwhile, were being kept back to face any possible British moves further along the Western Front.

On receiving this news, the Crown Prince began to doubt the High Command's commitment to operations at Verdun. Without its absolute backing, he felt, there was little point in going on. To this end he sought an audience with Falkenhayn, and the two met on 29 February. A frank exchange of views is reported to have taken place, during which Wilhelm made a number of demands of Falkenhayn, including reassurances that sufficient men and materials – 'not by driblets, but on a large scale' – be provided to sustain the offensive. Further, he expressed the opinion that the attack on Verdun should be terminated when 'we ourselves were losing more heavily and becoming exhausted more rapidly than the enemy'. Finally, he addressed the question of strategy. It was a matter of urgency that the attack be spread to encompass the weakest point of the Verdun defences, namely the left bank, to give a greater chance of a breakthrough and the 'relieving [of] our main attack on the eastern [i.e. right] bank from a harassing fire, which was hindering . . . further progress'.

The High Command's actual reply to these demands is not known but the Crown Prince must have received some or all of the assurances that he sought. He returned to his headquarters at Stenay that evening confident as ever, and imbued with a greater sense of purpose. Furthermore, Falkenhayn had relented on one crucial point and agreed to extend the offensive to the left bank of the Meuse. Pétain's gravest fears were about to come about. From early in March, the Germans would be attacking Verdun on both banks of the River Meuse simultaneously.

Throughout March, the battle in the air began to alter. These changes, however, had more to do with German tactical inertia than any radical re-thinking by the French. Certainly, the French air command had risen to the challenge presented by the enemy in the first few days of the attack. This coincided with the German air mission ceasing to compliment the efforts of the ground force, with its attacks over the French line yielding ever-diminishing returns. Moreover, a complete lack of tactical foresight was beginning to tell. A number of prime artillery targets – notably on the left bank – were left unscathed as the Germans started flying in predictable formations. In response, the French employed a more diverse and cunning approach which was soon reflected in an increased number of productive excursions.

The inability of the German command to direct attacks against the *Voie Sacrée* – which was about half an hour's flying time from the German air-field – proved to be a puzzling tactical blunder of some magnitude. The target was an obviously soft one. Its narrowness, and the fact that it ran largely across flat land, left it difficult to defend and particularly vulnerable to aerial attack. One small hit at any point along the way would have caused immeasurable damage to French operations at Verdun; a series of bigger hits would undoubtedly have changed the entire complexion of the battle and given the Germans a huge advantage. But, for whatever reasons, it was not to be.

Conversely, the French fought tenaciously to establish ascendancy in the skies above Verdun and, once this had been achieved, they battled just as hard to maintain it. Despite all the German technical superiority in the air, they seemed to lack the necessary *élan* to wage a successful aerial campaign. The French had it in apparently endless measure.

On 6 March, the attack across the rolling left-bank slopes in front of Verdun was preceded by a forceful artillery bombardment that, in its intensity, drew comparison with the onslaught of 21 February. The convergence point for this, and the following infantry advance, was the Mort Homme (or Dead Man). Named after a sinister and obscure medieval legend, the position was one of a twin of steep hills – the other being

Mort Homme

Le Mort Homme, a steep incline on the left bank of the River Meuse, was one of the most bitterly contested positions during the Battle of Verdun. This reflected its strategic significance – it was a superb observation post, providing an unrivalled panoramic view of the battlefield – and that it served as an excellent artillery position. It was from here that, in late February and early March 1916, French guns managed to inflict serious damage on the German infantry as it attempted to advance across the right bank.

Once the decision had been made to extend the offensive at Verdun to encompass the left bank, the German High Command had little choice other than to order an assault upon the slopes of Mort Homme. Not only would the position's capture debilitate the French artillery positions there, it was further calculated that all other left-bank defences would be left dangerously vulnerable to further attack.

In practice, the task of taking Mort Homme was a monumental one that took nearly three months to complete. This was in large part due to the logistical difficulties attached to overcoming a resilient defensive line camped out on higher ground. In early March, a blistering artillery and infantry attack was repelled by a determined French rearguard action. A second assault, on 14 March, was of an even more ferocious nature. Yet, despite some notable gains in the vicinity of Mort Homme, the position itself could not be taken. The French simply dug themselves in and weathered the storm. The process was repeated time and again until the summit of Mort Homme had been made altogether uninhabitable by either force. One attack, on 9 April, was believed by one eyewitness to represent the 'most savage' of any launched at Verdun in 1916.

Eventually the defence – which suffered increasingly from a lack of resources – became worn down by fatigue and the dogged determination of the repeated attacks. In late May, the Germans finally captured Mort Homme. But it is debatable whether the effort was worth it. Certainly, the Germans never managed to exploit occupancy of the site to the same extent that the French had. Nevertheless, they held on to the point, resisting all French counter-moves in January and March 1917. It was not until late August of that year that the French could once again proclaim Mort Homme as theirs. The entire operation took just four days, in stark contrast to the protracted battle of the previous spring.

Côte 304 – that reached a height of 295 metres and afforded a remarkable view of the surrounding countryside. Its strategic significance was enormous. The capture of the point would not only obliterate the shelter under which the French artillery on the left bank was firing but would also leave the defensive ground positions acutely exposed to any advancing line of attack.

A concerted offensive, it was believed, could bring Mort Homme under German control, hence the concentrated artillery effort. This was to be backed up by an infantry charge led by the as yet unused VI Reserve Corps which, it was decided, would be continuously reinforced to keep the strength of the attacking force at a steady six to eight divisions. At this point, General Bezelaire had four French divisions positioned variously across the left bank, with another one in reserve.

The effect of the artillery barrage was predictably devastating. French positions were directly hit, lives were indiscriminately claimed, and communications with the rear cut. Morale began to seep away. The Germans decided to exploit the effects of the barrage as quickly as possible and, within an hour of the bombardment lifting and before the French had enough time to regroup, the infantry proceeded in a

Memorial to the French dead of Mort Homme

Le Mort Homme: *'ils n'ont pas passé'*

The summit of Mort Homme – pictured here in the 1920s – was completely re-shaped by the battle for its possession in 1916

southerly direction across difficult terrain towards Mort Homme.

Initially, the tactic worked well. General von Zwehl, with a reserve division, the 22nd, made good ground against a weak defensive line. In time, the village of Forges – just across from the German infantry's initial point of departure – fell with little trouble, and was followed by the easterly lying settlement of Regneville. Further towards Mort Homme, some important tactical points were taken, including Height 265 which verged on its western side with the Bois des Corbeaux. In turn, this was on the north-eastern extreme of Mort Homme itself. The French were not completely outdone, however, and the artillery managed to ensure that the northern approaches to Mort Homme remained unassailed by the Germans.

Nevertheless, it took a little longer for the infantry to respond. The next day, under further artillery attack, the 67th Division crumbled and the Germans captured the Bois des Corbeaux, taking over 3000 prisoners in the process. The strategic advantage was now undisputedly with the attacking force as it closed in on its intended goal. Another costly catastrophe loomed large for the French at Verdun.

General Bezelaire swiftly announced the standard order to retake the lost ground. Led into the fray by the wily Lieutenant-Colonel Macker, the hastily assembled rearguard set out just before dawn on 8 March, in what may well have turned out to be another shameful example of the folly of *L'attaque à outrance*. But, uncharacteristically, the Germans were taken completely unawares, and a heroic bayonet-charge forced a general retreat. The smouldering Bois des Corbeaux was, perhaps surprisingly, retaken. Suddenly forced into taking a backward step, for the rest of the day the German line had to concentrate on holding those gains made so far. The general offensive on the left bank was, in the meantime, called to a temporary halt.

With the Germans forced to consolidate, and the French ensuring that their 'Line of Resistance' on the left bank was upheld, the action in this region abated for a time, save for some relatively low-key artillery manoeuvres. Over the next few days, some small and vicious attacks and counter-attacks characterized the fighting to the north of Mort Homme. On 10 March, a German offensive push enabled them to recapture the Bois des Corbeaux but this served simply to disguise the fact that something of a stalemate had developed on the left bank.

Meanwhile, there had been a full-blown re-engagement of activity on the opposing bank of the Meuse. This was no coincidence but, rather, a planned simultaneous attack along the eastern extreme of the right bank towards Fort Vaux which had begun to menace the German line following its reinforcement in late February. The intended effect, however, was lessened because logistical problems, involving moving ammunition supplies up to the front, meant that the offensive had to be postponed for 48 hours. Consequently, the advantage the Crown Prince had sought to create across the whole of the sector did not quite materialize as planned.

Nevertheless, when the artillery eventually opened up, it was deadly and included some gas shells. Stationed within Fort Vaux, one eyewitness noted that the bombardment was intense and drawn out: 'It was like dwelling under a sledge-hammer', he noted, 'or having someone's fist planted in the pit of one's stomach.' He went on:

> . . . imagine solid blocks of eight hundred or nine hundred kilograms com-
> ing from a distance of twelve to fifteen kilometres, rising to a height of four
> or five thousand metres and breaking just above one's head, discharging
> their devastating contents of sixty or eighty kilograms of high explosive.
> We were stunned every time, and after a few hours of it our nerves were al-
> most shattered . . .

On the battlefield, the dead and wounded lay everywhere. Henry Bor-
deaux observed that a 'nameless stench rises from the tortured soil'. The scene was, by now, the familiar one. As he wrote:

> The countryside looks scorched and burnt. The lava of a volcano, the shocks
> of an earthquake, all the cataclysms of nature would not have flayed it more
> unmercifully. It is a chaos without a name, a circle in Dante's inferno.

The German infantry was able to advance across this frenzied soil, reach-
ing the village of Vaux – which was to change hands some thirteen times in March alone – and the grounds of the fort itself for little effort. But, thereafter, the advance petered out, becoming immediately bogged down in heavy fighting. Across this strip of land the two sides interlocked. Amid the ensuing chaos and carnage, reports began to filter back, indicating that the attacking force had made some notable gains. The validity of these claims was not checked, however, and on 9 March, an official German communiqué announced to the world that its forces had 'taken by assault the armoured Fort Vaux, as well as numerous neighbouring fortifications'.

Somewhat embarrassingly, the claim was quickly shown to be a false one. Immediately, French propagandists seized on the mistake as proof of German profligacy on the battlefield as well as the rising strength of the French defences. Joffre used it as an excuse to congratulate the French forces at Verdun, announcing in an Order of the Day on 10 March, that:

> For three weeks you have withstood the most formidable attack which the
> enemy has yet made. Germany counted on the success of this effort, which
> she believed would prove irresistible, and for which she used her best
> troops and most powerful artillery. She hoped by the capture of Verdun to
> strengthen the courage of her Allies and convince neutrals of German su-
> periority. But she reckoned without you! The eyes of the country are on
> you. You belong to those of whom it will be said: 'They barred the road to
> Verdun.'

Pétain, however, refused to get carried away and remained far more level headed in his analysis of the battle. On the same day he telegraphed Joffre, warning him that: 'The enemy attacks are more and more violent; we cannot face up to them unless the influx of resources is continuous'. But Joffre was not likely to become overly concerned so long as the German advance was held in abeyance on both banks of the Meuse.

The following day the first attempted Allied diversionary tactic, discussed in December 1915 at Chantilly and intended to relieve some of the pressure on the French at Verdun, saw the Italians attacking once more along the Isonzo front. The impact was minimal but much appreciated all the same and, for the Germans, was a telling foretaste of what was to come.

On 14 March, the 'frenzied duel' around Mort Homme picked up pace. On a sunny, spring-like day, six crack German divisions made another significant thrust towards the hill and the French positions in the vicinity of it. Once started, this renewed campaign was to take on a relentless, sinister momentum of its own. It would be nearly two months before the ferocity of the battle here abated.

The Germans set no limits for the attack. The necessary men and materials were made available for the renewed effort against Mort Homme. Croisilles witnessed, 'Innumerable enemy shells [which] shrill the air with the screech of missiles, plaintive and prolonged whistlings, dull rumblings and deafening reports'. For almost two weeks the German tactical approach remained steadfast: hours of artillery barrage that fired the skies above Verdun blood red, followed by an attempted infantry breakthrough. Day after day, the French resisted with equal measures of bravery and heroism. With woodlands razed, combat took place mostly in the open, with attackers and defenders alike forced to take shelter in dank and dangerous shell holes.

There was little respite from either side, and the battle ebbed and flowed for some time, with both forces launching heavy assaults. As hand-to-hand combatants, grenadiers, and machine-gunners worked away at the foot of Mort Homme, the summit itself was under a constant torrent of shells that would soon render it altogether uninhabitable. By the end of March, total German casualties – comprising the dead, wounded and 'missing' – had passed the 80,000 mark; French losses were closer to 90,000.

Throughout this time, French machine-gunners were achieving considerable success from the peak of Côte 304, due west of Mort Homme. The German line was taking severe punishment from this lofty ridge, and this caused the Fifth Army's command to decide on a change of tactics.

Unless the position was knocked out, it was realized, there was little chance of mounting a successful advance on Mort Homme. Moreover, they could no longer sustain such a high rate of casualties for little or no gain (on one day alone, some 2400 men were lost to the war effort). The position was approached from an extreme westerly direction through the Bois d'Avocourt and the village of Malancourt. The 11th Bavarian Division was thrown into the fray and, on 20 March, inflicted heavy losses on the French defence concentrated in and around the Bois d'Avocourt. The wood, which under German planning was a vital key to Côte 304, was then overrun as the exhausted defending force of the French 29th Division was crushed in a little over four hours. Some 2800 troops, with a number of machine-guns and cannons, were captured by the Germans. To the French the blow was a critical one, not just for morale but, more importantly, in terms of strategy. There now existed a gaping hole in the defensive position that threatened the entire left-bank 'Line of Resistance'.

The sense of disgrace attached to any such military collapse was heightened in this instance by evidence of double-dealing – or, at least, some form of complicity with the Germans – from within the French camp. Suspicions had been aroused by the precision with which the Germans had infiltrated the heavily defended wood. Furthermore, the readiness with which the substantial defensive force had surrendered cast additional doubt on the line's loyalty but insufficient proof existed to solve the question decisively.

Nonetheless, the loss had a stinging effect, and the French were provoked into taking serious retributive action. Consequently, the full weight of the left-bank artillery was brought to bear on the Bois d'Avocourt. On 29 March, in a dashing counter-move, part of the wood was retaken but only at an enormous cost. For their part, despite the fatigue suffered from being engaged in the battle zone for too long, the German infantry were able to consolidate throughout the rest of the Bois d'Avocourt and, as March gave way to April, begin to exploit the gaps in the defensive line. On 31 March, Malancourt was the first of a number of villages to fall before the attacking force. Six days later, Haucourt capitulated, followed by Bethincourt on 8 April.

Once again, the French started to panic, not only because of the severity of their losses, but also owing to the sheer tenacity of the German onslaught. It appeared as if they meant to break through on the left bank whatever the cost. Even Joffre became concerned. The same day as Bethincourt fell, the General Staff telegraphed an increasingly exasperated Pétain, ordering 'a vigorous offensive to be undertaken with the least possible delay'.

The village of Malancourt in ruins following the German push across the left bank in March 1916

As far as the Germans were concerned, the stakes had now become too high to justify any other course of action than a relentless pursual of the offensive. The attacking force was suffering enormous losses – not so much bleeding as haemorrhaging – but this could now be justified because the Germans had not yet reached the point where their losses exceeded those of the enemy. This cold calculation absolved any need for further vindication. The German High Command appeared to believe that quantity rather than quality would ultimately win the battle.

As outlined in his memorandum to the Kaiser, the secondary prong of Falkenhayn's proposed strategy for indirectly attacking the British in 1916 was an indiscriminate campaign of submarine warfare across the naval and sea-trade approaches to the British Isles. Hitherto, the campaign had been relatively low key but had resulted in some notable success and seemed as if it might yet yield significant dividends.

On 24 March, however, it was abruptly called off by Wilhelm II. That day, a French civilian passenger ship, the *Sussex*, sailing from Newhaven to Dieppe – and carrying among its passengers a number of American civilians and journalists – was torpedoed as it crossed the English Channel.

Immediately, the United States threatened to sever diplomatic relations with Germany if the episode was repeated and the campaign not called off immediately.

In the face of such pressure, the Kaiser felt he had no other choice than to relent. With the weight of numbers already working against the Central Powers, Wilhelm II could not take the chance of provoking a row with the Americans. Consequently, German submarines were thereafter instructed to target only legitimate military vessels.

Throughout March, the Germans engaged at Verdun had been paying an ever heavier price in human life for each minor success. Therefore, the High Command was increasingly less than impressed by each new report on battle casualty statistics. By April, there was evidence that Falkenhayn's objective in bleeding the French at Verdun was diminishing in proportion to the increase in German casualties there. At Stenay, however, the belief continued to prevail 'that the fate of the French army would be decided by the issue of the Battle of Verdun', and the Crown Prince remained as determined as ever 'to employ every possible means at our disposal of using up the enemy's effective reserves alike of troops, munitions and material'.

So once again, the offensive along the entire Verdun front was stepped up. On the right bank, where the defensive line was strongest, the situation was to remain a fairly static one for some time. Now under General von Mudra's overall command along this flank, the Germans pressed forward continually, making small gains here and there but all the time paying a high human price for them. The French casualty list was hardly any shorter as they continued vigorously to counter all German moves. The overall pattern remained largely unchanged and the suffering and killing went on unabated.

The German command was confident that the left bank still represented the best chance for achieving a quick and decisive breakthrough. It was at this point, therefore, that the offensive effort became mainly concentrated. Following the failure to take Côte 304, the new German head of operations on the left bank, General von Gallwitz, was forced by a wavering and impatient High Command to make a tactical switch – which he did not agree with – and revert to a direct attempt to capture Mort Homme.

For the whole of 8 April, the position was the focus for an artillery bombardment of almost unprecedented severity. A French officer who experienced the German onslaught that day dubbed it 'a second beginning of the struggle on the forty-ninth day'. The defensive line knew exactly what the barrage indicated. The same officer later recalled:

The Mort-Homme smoked like a volcano with innumerable craters. Before and behind, our barrages and those of the Germans looked like curtains of flame . . . In the air floated the ugly green puffs of smoke which told of 150's and 130's. The earth trembled under the incessant cannonade. The assault which was in preparation was destined to be one of the most savage of the battle of Verdun.

The prediction proved to be correct. Early the next morning, the XXII German Reserve Corps, led by Falkenhayn's elder brother and childhood tutor to the Crown Prince, Eugene, advanced towards the battered but unyielding Mort Homme. Progress was slow under a shower of shells and gunfire. Furthermore, the infantry was exhausted, and the elder Falkenhayn clearly shared his brother's cautious nature. Despite fatalities and the wounded being steadily replaced from a heavy supporting line throughout the advance, the Germans could move on only as far as a northerly crest of Mort Homme, perhaps a little over three-quarters of the way up the steep incline. At one point, the attacking command believed that the summit of the hill had been reached, only for another steep ridge shortly to appear in the near distance.

By now, the French line was severely under-resourced. Reservists were being requested from all points along the line but there was none to call upon. Despite Pétain's best efforts, Joffre adamantly refused to release any fresh divisions for the relief of Verdun. Ever-tighter restrictions were being enforced across the sector because of the necessity, as Joffre saw it, of observing the broader strategic picture along the Western Front.

This did not stop the General Staff urging Pétain to maintain an 'aggressive attitude'. A communiqué despatched from Mort Homme by the commander of the 8th Battalion, Captain de Surrain, on the night of 9 April, appeared to render this last command unnecessary. He reported that:

They [the troops under his command] are doing all they can to hold their ground. The men know the seriousness of the situation, but their *morale* remains good. They are resolved to die rather than give way . . . You may rest assured that every man has done his whole duty.

In an Order of the Day, Pétain praised the stalwart defence of Mort Homme, claiming 9 April as 'a glorious day for our forces'. He then enjoined: '*Courage, on les aura!*' (Courage, we shall have them yet!)

The next day brought an attempted infantry counter-move from the French. Under the circumstances, it seemed to be doomed from the outset. Advancing under a murderous hail of machine-gun fire, the

Germans were able to inflict the maximum number of casualties upon the French force, annihilating line after line of men. Dead bodies littered the shell-scarred slopes of Mort Homme, as another round of futile sacrifice was suffered. These were losses that the French could hardly afford to suffer. Not for the first time at Verdun, however, providence intervened to avert the infliction of unsustainable carnage upon the French defence. The heavens opened in a torrent of rain that was ultimately to cause the suspension of all offensive operations in the direction of Mort Homme. The deluge lasted some twelve days, turning the battle zone into a swamp.

The hiatus afforded the French the opportunity to survey the full extent of the damages recently wrought by the enemy. One retiring Captain, Augustin Cochin, noted on 14 April that, 'I arrived here with 175 men, I return with 34, several of them half crazy'. On the same day, the commander of the 151st Regiment was reduced to operating with ten competent men but was still turned down when he requested reinforcements, being told in no uncertain terms that there was none available.

It seemed that the pressure of living under such intense conditions had affected the mental stability of many of the defenders at Mort Homme. Many were numbed by all that was unfolding about them. From his vantage point, an artilleryman witnessed innumerable *poilus* situated 'only just' behind the line at Mort Homme – that is, within striking distance of the deadliest battle zone at Verdun at this time – 'strolling about apparently unconcerned, as if this [battle] was an entirely normal occurrence'. A bizarre sight, undoubtedly, but, after being subjected to the incessant inferno for so long, perhaps it really was a 'normal occurrence' for many Frenchmen.

The French line on both banks of the Meuse held throughout April, but only just. A renewed onslaught in early May finally cracked the 'Line of Resistance' along the left bank. Everywhere outnumbered and outgunned, and with morale reaching a new low, more of the same gruelling bombardment proved too much for the harassed defenders of Mort Homme. Working at full tilt, the German artillery opened up on 3 May. For two days and two nights more than 500 high-calibre artillery pieces continuously pounded away at the French line. The defensive artillery batteries there, which had recently proven so effective, were all but knocked out. Nevertheless, the defending infantry inflicted much damage on the opposition but could not prevent the fall of Côte 304.

Each side was now inflicting upon the other enormous casualties. Entire regiments were disappearing under accurate volleys of shells and showers of bullets. Replacements disappeared in a similar fashion often only minutes after falling into line. Some estimates suggest that, by early May, German losses were for the first time exceeding those of the French.

Whether this was the case is a moot point but it was a close-run thing. Certainly, the Germans were not helped by a mass explosion within the confines of Fort Douaumont on 8 May, caused when a fire in one ammunition deposit began a chain reaction. The accident claimed about 650 lives.

After the loss of Côte 304, the French position on the left bank began slowly but inexorably to crumble. The French rearguard was valiant but, with less than adequate resources in every sense, the bolstered German advance simply proved irresistible. Mort Homme finally changed hands after the most bitter of struggles; by the end of the month so had the village of Cumières – another settlement erased from the map. All that the defenders had managed to do was postpone the inevitable through a series of costly counter-moves.

With the left-bank resistance effectively – albeit temporarily – curtailed, the Germans could now concentrate the full weight of their efforts against Verdun upon the intransigent right-bank positions. But for how much longer the soldiers of both armies could put up with the continual strains being placed on them was open to question. A 21-year-old lieutenant, serving the French in the 124th Regiment, confided to his diary on 23 May:

> Humanity is mad! It must be mad to do what it is doing. What a massacre. What scenes of horror and carnage! I cannot find words to translate my impressions. Hell cannot be so terrible. Men are mad!

Within two days he was dead, another victim of Verdun's hell.

7

Symbol of Struggle and Freedom

> Verdun had become more than a battle;
> now it was a symbol of struggle and freedom.
> Lyn Macdonald, *The Roses of No Man's Land*

THE WAR OF attrition that unfolded in worsening measures at Verdun throughout March, April, and May 1916 cost both armies dearly. But, in truth, the general situation on the battlefield had been little altered by the end of it. The Germans were advancing in metres not kilometres; the French were still managing a tenable defence of the city. Yet both sides were clearly struggling to sustain the huge efforts required of them. The Germans had not planned for such heavy losses and could surely not go on at the same level indefinitely. On the other hand, the fighting strength of the French was stretched to the limit and this, ahead of the planned joint action with the British on the Somme, would inevitably strain limited resources still further. Sooner or later, something – in a strategic sense – would have to give.

In psychological terms, it was now a question of who cracked first. Falkenhayn observed that 'this fighting without visible or – for the man at the front – tangible result afforded the sternest test imaginable of the capabilities of the troops'. Most of those on the spot – and Croisilles was one of them – believed the Battle of Verdun to represent the 'frontiers of humanity, frontiers which at any moment we may overpass'. The *Vossiche Zeitung* in Germany offered an incisive commentary on the matter:

> The battle of Verdun is not a human battle at all. It is hell. A man needs a devil in him to be able to survive it. No human beings can be expected to tear away whole rows of barbed wire and escape the snares of all sorts and the pitiless machine-guns. The attacking [German] forces have only death, carnage, and horror before them. We are fighting against an enemy who is a match for us. In men and material . . . he is our equal. No secret of modern warfare is unknown to the French.

Realistically, any kind of denouement under such conditions seemed a long way off. For the foreseeable future, both sides seemed likely to

A German observation post on the left bank at Montfaucon

Remains of the church, Montfaucon

continue to bleed (one estimate suggests that, by the end of April, German losses exceeded 120,000 compared with French casualties of some 133,000).

At least the French could take some satisfaction from the fact that they continued to hold Verdun and fend off the offensive force. Fort Douaumont apart, all strategic losses across the line had been adequately absorbed, and the actual threat to the sector was not proportionally much more marked at the end of May than it had been at the end of February.

The Germans could take no such comfort from closer analysis of their performance to that time. The full-scale offensive on the left bank had shown only a limited return. Certainly, the strategically important Mort Homme had been captured and the dangerous French artillery positions around there knocked out. But this still left them some 10 kilometres or so from Verdun, across terrain that was both hostile and difficult. On the right bank, little had tangibly altered since the beginning of March. Initiative was passing alternately between the two sides but the frequency and severity of these skirmishes were costing the Germans a disproportionately high number of men.

It was the opinion of many that the Germans were paying the price for not attacking sooner across both banks of the Meuse simultaneously. The earlier denial of reinforcements was also seen as a key tactical error. If it had been Falkenhayn's intention to bleed the French at Verdun at a minimal cost, the plan had clearly come undone as German casualties mounted ever higher. The truth of the matter was that Falkenhayn's caution – or indecision, depending on one's viewpoint – had, on a number of occasions, resulted in the initiative passing from German hands at the vital moment.

The Germans were now faced with an important strategic choice regarding Verdun. Should they continue with Falkenhayn's 'bleeding' experiment, at a time when the plan's architect appeared to be losing some interest in it, or should they cut their losses? The latter option was surreptitiously proposed by the Crown Prince towards the end of April. He suggested that the offensive be curtailed while some semblance of German prestige remained intact. In his war memoirs, he wrote:

> I was now convinced, after the stubborn to and fro contest for every foot of ground which had continued throughout the whole of April, that although we had more than once changed our methods of attack, a decisive success at Verdun could only be assured at the price of heavy sacrifices, out of all proportion to the desired gains. I naturally came to this conclusion only with the greatest reluctance; it was no easy matter for me, the responsible commander, to abandon my dreams of hope and victory!

Unfortunately for the commander of the Fifth Army, he had little influence where it mattered most, with his father, so there was only ever a slim chance that his opinion would prevail.

Nevertheless, his view seemed eminently sensible to many, and drew the broad support of all members bar one of the Fifth's operational staff. The exception was the Army's Chief of Staff, General Konstantin Schmidt von Knobelsdorf. Renowned as a strong personality, Knobelsdorf arguably had more overall power than the Crown Prince throughout the Fifth Army and, indeed, to many the latter was merely a nepotistic and pampered figurehead of little importance. Whether this was fully justified or not does not diminish the *de facto* reality of Knobelsdorf's will-power and the weight his opinion carried, especially with the Kaiser. Furthermore, it was he who had reputedly sown in Falkenhayn's mind the seed of the idea for the attack on Verdun. Consequently, by May, he was possibly the most rabid advocate of the 'bleeding' plan and, as such, came to see himself more and more as – in the words of Horne – 'the organiser of victory at Verdun'.

So it was Knobelsdorf who, despite his theoretically subordinate status, came to have the final say on the matter. It was his belief that, as matters stood, national honour dictated the capture of Verdun and, consequently, he backed the mounting of a heavy assault against France's right-bank positions. To facilitate this policy further, he set about altering the composition of the Fifth Army's staff, replacing known supporters of the Crown Prince's position with his own men. Consequently, Knobelsdorf's personal staff officer, von Heymann, was transferred to Verdun, and General von Mudra – the perceived pessimist in command of the right-bank sector – was replaced by General von Lochow hitherto commander of the III Brandenburger Corps.

There was broad support throughout the military, and from politicians, for Knobelsdorf's stance. It was widely thought that, if nothing else, keeping the French engaged at Verdun would limit their ability to participate effectively in the forthcoming Franco-British offensive along the Western Front which was now widely anticipated by all the Central Powers. In civilian circles, support could be a little less subtle. The Stuttgart press aired the view that the German goal at Verdun must remain steadfast, and that nothing less than 'the final and utter destruction of the forces of our enemies' would do.

On the French side, a divergence of opinion between Pétain and Joffre over the strategy to be pursued at Verdun, slowly built into an open conflict. Their differing philosophical standpoints on military matters had meant that relations between the two were, at best, cool. Now, during the crucial spring months at Verdun, they had moved even further apart to a point where a schism had clearly developed.

Pétain, who was becoming by the day increasingly emotionally drained by the strain of the battle, resented Joffre's cool pronouncements on the situation at Verdun, made always from a geographically removed

The remains of the church at Avacourt, site of fierce fighting in late March 1916

position. He – together with the rest of his staff and the majority of the French fighting force – did not totally believe that, through relayed official communiqués, the General Staff could comprehend fully the severity of the situation at Verdun. But, at this time, this was an accepted fact of military life and, as such, was only a minor complaint. The thrust of the argument concerned where, in terms of human and material resources, the French Army's priorities lay for the year 1916.

Joffre was adamant that the army's, and the country's, main concern was the coming action on the Somme. He referred to Verdun – correctly but rather chillingly in the light of what was unfolding there – as 'only one incident in the general struggle'. Consequently, he would give to the fight at Verdun only 'a strict minimum of forces', in other words, the least he possibly could. He would not countenance suggestions that any other procedure should be followed for a battle of attrition from which he 'could hope to obtain no strategic results whatever'.

Pétain could not fully comprehend this stance. It seemed to him slightly imprudent to intertwine France's fate with that of another ally – albeit a major one – who, as far as he understood matters, was not wholly trustworthy and had only just begun to pull its full weight in the war effort on continental Europe. If France was to have any hope, he argued, it must put its own affairs in order first, and that meant concentrating all efforts for the year on the defence of Verdun.

In essence, it was this rift that led to endless squabbling between the commander of the Second Army and the French Commander-in-Chief throughout March and April. Pétain was forever requesting more reserves, Joffre forever denying them to him. When Pétain inquired after new cannons and other field guns, he was informed that Joffre was having them transferred directly from factory to the Somme region ahead of the planned offensive there.

There were other fundamental differences of opinion, mostly concerning the way in which Pétain was conducting operations at Verdun. Joffre believed the French needed to adopt a more thoroughly aggressive stance at Verdun. He thought that it 'was most essential for us to take and keep the initiative. In my opinion this was the most efficacious method of preventing the enemy from making any further progress.' He felt his commander at Verdun 'had not sufficiently grasped this idea'. Joffre wrote further:

> In contact as he was with the daily realities of this violent battle and constantly menaced by new attacks, he showed too marked a tendency, perhaps an attribute of his temperament, to look upon the defensive as the only possible attitude.

Such an attitude – whether or not it really existed – was, of course, anathema to all that Joffre believed in. Consequently, he wished to replace Pétain not long after his appointment at Verdun. Slowly, as relations between the two soured, Joffre increasingly felt the need to urge Pétain on towards the seemingly obvious, such as 'the need of striking back . . . [of recovering] little by little, the ground we had lost'. Pétain, however, would not be swayed in his belief that, in the context of Verdun, such a philosophy was completely unrealistic, especially as he was being denied, on an almost daily basis, the necessary men and materials for such operations.

Nevertheless, Pétain continued to order whatever counter-attacks he thought had a chance of succeeding. But, from Joffre's point of view, these did not suffice and, in consequence, the two were unable to form a viable working relationship. Georges Blond expounds the notion that, at heart, the clash was one of personality, 'between military doctrine and human feeling'. In the end, Joffre began to view Pétain's caution as a sign of deep-rooted pessimism. Annoyed by his refusal to launch any kind of major counter-stroke against the Germans – who, he felt, were being allowed too much scope for dictating the pace and direction of the battle – Joffre ultimately came to regret installing Pétain at Verdun.

But removing him would be no straightforward task. Ignorant as it was of the nuances of the operation at Verdun, French public opinion had been made all too well aware that the General had played a decisive role in averting catastrophe and national humiliation at Verdun at the end of February. As a result, he was popularly fêted across France as the Saviour of Verdun. Joffre did not even attempt to overcome this problem; he merely bypassed it. In late April, he removed Pétain from the scene at Verdun by 'promoting' him to the post of Commander of Central Armies Group Headquarters. He was replaced at the head of the Second Army by General Robert Nivelle.

In retrospect, Joffre justified his decision by playing upon Pétain's obvious strategical limitations. He wrote that he withdrew the General from Verdun, hoping that such a move would afford him 'a more distant perspective, a wider front upon which to direct his action . . . a clearer view'. Outwardly, Pétain accepted the promotion with good grace but secretly felt it to be nothing other than a blatant dismissal. He vented his feelings, in no uncertain terms, in a personal letter to the future Minister of War, Painlevé.

Inasmuch as he shared Joffre's military principles, Nivelle was more orthodox in his outlook. He was certainly offensively minded in terms of tactics, and stated the belief that continual attacks on a large scale could bring the war to a speedy end. Immediately after arriving at Verdun, he was stressing 'the many possibilities open to those who take the aggressive'. Evidently, Joffre had his man. Ambitious and self-confident, Nivelle's rise through the ranks of the French Army had been accelerated by the war. He was well regarded in military and in political circles, and had a natural charm that tended to captivate people of influence.

His right-hand man, Charles Mangin, was reputedly one of the fiercest generals in all the French Army. He was also an advocate of the offensive – perhaps more so than any of his contemporaries – reflecting his love of a good fight. Something of an old-fashioned swashbuckler, Mangin – rarely for a French general of his generation – could often be seen leading by example from the front, keeping the tightest of controls on the actions of his command. His combative maxim was, 'One must bite first in order not to be bitten', and this was reflected, in spirit, to the troops of Verdun in one of his first Orders of the Day, published in late April:

No Frenchman can rest as long as a savage enemy treads the sacred soil of our country; there can be no peace for the world until the monster of Prussian militarism is overthrown. So you will ready yourselves for new combats, to which you will bring the conviction of your superiority, having seen the enemy raise his hands or flee before your bayonets and your grenades.

'The butcher', General Mangin

On handing over command to Nivelle, Pétain is reported to have said, 'General, my watchword when the battle broke out was: they will not pass. I hand it on to you'. Thereafter, a new broom swept through the French line at Verdun. As an early example of this, the system of the *Noria* was slowed considerably. Pétain, meanwhile, was charged with overseeing from afar the entire Verdun war effort. His brief was to ensure 'the inviolability of our positions', and more specifically, to mastermind a plan to recapture the fort at Douaumont.

The debate among the hierarchy of the German Army and the fractures evident within the French staff were indicative of the fact that Verdun had taken on a heavy symbolic significance out of all proportion to its actual strategic importance, which had always been a point of some contention. As Falkenhayn had correctly predicted, national honour was compelling France to hold out at Verdun regardless of the ultimate cost. Likewise,

Germany's military credibility along the Western Front had become entwined with the ultimate capture of the city. For either side, no outcome other than outright victory would suffice, once Joffre for the French and Knobelsdorf for the Germans had got their respective ways regarding the future conduct of the battle. Consequently, both parties were prepared to battle on regardless of the human and material sacrifices which no one seemed to be counting that closely any longer. Alistair Horne has written:

> In their determination to possess this symbol, this challenge-cup of national supremacy, the two nations flailed at each other with all the stored-up rage of a thousand years of Teuton-Gaul rivalry . . . [It] was [now] more than simply the honour, it was the virility of the two peoples that was at stake. Like two stags battling to the death, antlers locked, neither would nor could give until the virility of one or the other finally triumphed.

Undeniably, the battle was becoming ever more brutal in nature. By the end of May, it was characterized by a quite desperate ferocity and, during the summer months, would enter its most lethal stage yet. The fighting assumed a deadly impetus all of its own, with the combatants on the ground seemingly having little control over the course of events. The infantry and artillery of both armies had now been fully committed to a deadly dog-eat-dog war of bitter attrition. The Germans pushed on relentlessly, as if it was the only thing they knew. The French, having for so long suffered the enemy's brutal tactical methods, countered and attacked relentlessly and without scruple. Antlers had indeed been tightly locked.

8

Towards Denouement

O ancient crimson curse!
Corrode, consume;
Give back this universe
Its pristine bloom.
Isaac Rosenberg,
On Receiving News of the War

IN THEORY, at least, the new French command at Verdun was formidable. It remained to be seen, however, whether Nivelle and Mangin's collective strength of character and self-confidence could be transmitted to the troops across the battle zone. With the Germans prepared to dig in for victory, far greater efforts still would be required from the defensive forces if the enemy were finally to be seen off.

In a military sense, Nivelle was very much a product of his time. The son of a French Army officer and an Englishwoman, he was born on 15 October 1856. Nivelle was educated at the École Polytechnique, passing out in 1878 before joining the French artillery. His formative military years took him to the Far East where, in 1900, he served in the repression of the Boxer Rebellion. As a Lieutenant-Colonel, he had spent some years in northern Africa.

Nivelle's reputation as a strong leader, imbued with great vision and cunning, was established during the early stages of World War I. As head of the 4th Artillery Regiment, he oversaw the defence of Mulhouse before excelling on the Marne with a surprise attack that decimated the advancing enemy infantry line. Thereafter, he rose to the rank of Brigadier-General before taking command of a division in early 1915. By the year's end, Nivelle was a Major-General, in command of the III Corps.

It was Verdun that spread his reputation throughout the whole of France and beyond. His effective organization of the line according to prevailing French military doctrine, and the introduction of new techniques of battle – which, many observers believed, would win the war for the allies – ultimately brought the French some unlikely successes at

General Nivelle, who replaced Pétain as commander of French
forces at Verdun on 1 May 1916

Verdun. And they also served to open the way for Nivelle to attain further
promotion.

In 1916, it was only Nivelle's timely intervention that saved his trusted
colleague, Charles Mangin, from obscurity following the swift demise in
battle of a number of colonial divisions under his command. Ominously
nicknamed by the *poilus* 'the butcher', Mangin was born on 6 July 1866 in
a part of Lorraine that had been annexed by Germany in the aftermath of
the Franco-Prussian War. Nevertheless, he retained French nationality
and entered military school. Upon graduation in 1888, he served for a
long period as an infantry officer throughout various parts of the French
empire. His early career was a most eventful and distinguished one, and he
was wounded in action on a number of occasions. Following various

stints in Africa – during one of which he led an expedition that took three years to cross the entire continent in a west–east direction – he spent a further three years in Indo-China.

On the outbreak of the war, Mangin was appointed a General and took command of a division of the Fifth Army, going on to participate in the 1915 offensives. It was during this time that his reputation as a brave and aggressive commander was established beyond doubt. It was also this period that gave rise to his macabre epithet for he became widely renowned as one who was not afraid to sustain unduly heavy losses. At Verdun, he commanded the 5th Division throughout the first months of the battle, overseeing the pursual of some of the bloodiest, most futile counter-attacks of the entire campaign.

With these two effectively at the helm, there was little chance that the deadly scenario which now engulfed Verdun was likely to recede. The destruction and the killing were a daily monotony across the whole war zone at Verdun. Nothing that now happened was liable to shock either the German or the French forces there. By this stage, both armies were inured to the horrors occurring all about them. The physical damage wrought to the landscape had also reached the point where it was now irreversible. From his aircraft, an American volunteer pilot of the Lafayette Squadron, James R. McConnell, noted of the battlefield:

> It seems to belong to another world. Every sign of humanity has swept away. The woods and the roads have vanished like chalk wiped from a blackboard; of the villages nothing remains but gray [*sic*] smears where stone walls have tumbled together. The great forts of Douaumont and Vaux are outlined faintly, like the tracings of a finger in wet sand. One cannot distinguish any one shell crater. . . Of the trenches only broken, half-obliterated links are visible.

This was the hell of Verdun, which descended a little further each day into the abyss. Yet there was more – much more – to come.

In an analysis of the strategic situation as it stood, Nivelle saw clearly that all French counter-moves on the right bank of the Meuse were failing in large part because of the German occupancy of Fort Douaumont. No one could have predicted just how dearly the French would pay in lives for this loss. Since capturing it, the Germans had used the fort to its full capacity, wreaking havoc for kilometres around in every direction. As one French artilleryman succinctly noted, 'They dominate us from Fort Douaumont'.

Since, in late February, Pétain had called a halt to efforts to retake it, it

An interior passageway, Fort Douaumont

had become ever more imperative that the French took back the position from the enemy. But, throughout March and April, there had existed neither the opportunity nor the resources to mount such an assault. It was realised that, to succeed, a feasible plan must be hatched and, thereafter, applied methodically. One attempt – hastily planned and prematurely executed – had been spearheaded by Mangin on 22 April. The outcome was a predictable, bloody failure. Mangin would not be so easily deterred, however, and, following the disaster within the walls of Fort Douaumont on 8 May, he decided to take advantage of the clear opportunity that this presented.

The effects of the explosion had left the occupants of the fort in disarray. The sheer force of the detonations had left no one unaffected because everything had been lifted into the air and thrown some distance. A doctor, Hallauer, stationed in the fort, told of the carnage created by the incident. The passageways were crammed with prostrate corpses, 'many of them hideously deformed. Arms, legs and body trunks lay everywhere; between them, smashed war material. The bodies of many of the dead, heaped three or four high, had been ripped open.' Many of those not killed outright suffered mortal shrapnel wounds, or died of asphyxiation from powerful gas releases and smoke. The scene was simply too horrific for many of the survivors to bear and pushed them 'to the edge of human resistance'. One officer, in the depths of depression brought on by the incident, shot himself through the head.

It would take some time to clear up the mess created by the blast and psychologically to come to terms with it. In the interim, the fort's garrison would be badly overstretched and under-resourced. It was this situation that Mangin planned to exploit. The new command at Verdun needed an early success to prove that it meant business, that it intended to adopt and sustain a more aggressive stance towards the enemy. This looked like a golden opportunity.

One historian has labelled the May offensive against Fort Douaumont, 'an act of desperation, based on an absolute imperative of instant results'. Mangin perceived it rather as amounting to nothing other than an 'absolute necessity'. The order for the attack was given by Nivelle in mid-May. Within hours, German intelligence had discovered enough about the plan to ensure that all efforts now switched from the general offensive to bulwarking the fort's defences. Consequently, any chance of a French success had been swiftly and severely diminished.

For the attack, the French concentrated upon Fort Douaumont their most formidable array of artillery yet seen in the battle. Some 300 heavy guns – including four 370-mm mortar pieces – pounded away at the position almost without ceasing for five days. The infantry, which was nowhere near as strong in depth as the artillery, advanced on 22 May, with two regiments proceeding along a narrow front of barely a kilometre in width.

The effects of the artillery barrage had been keenly felt within the structure of the fort, and gave rise to a certain amount of trepidation among the garrison. This was not lessened by the fact that communications had been adversely affected and observation posts knocked out. Furthermore, the troops holding the fort were living under the most inhumane of conditions. The capability of the Germans to counter the attack from outside the fort remained largely undiminished, however, and the existing arsenal within it still worked effectively enough.

Consequently, on approaching the fortification, the advancing French line was subjected to a brutal storm of gunfire that resulted in whole battalions being ravaged and, in one case, wiped out altogether. The 129th Division, which was supposed to storm the fort, was quickly reduced to only forty-five able-bodied troops; the 74th Battalion never managed to leave its trench, so ferocious was the barrage ahead of it. The German gunners were working with brutal precision. Attacking from flanking positions, German machine-guns relentlessly cut swathes through row after row of advancing *poilus*.

Nevertheless, the guns were powerless to keep all the marching line at bay, and some French infantry, led by the 34th Regiment, reached the perimeter of the fort in just a few minutes. Subsequently, under a menacing artillery volley, French forces were able to exploit some of the gaps rendered upon the fortification. Over the course of the day, isolated parties managed steadily to penetrate the fort from various directions. One group made it into the heart of the structure, reaching the central rampart; another succeeded in taking control of a machine-gun turret. By nightfall, well over half of Fort Douaumont was back in French hands, the occupants having retreated to the fort's lower level.

At this point, the signs for the French were good and it looked as though the position might be completely retaken. Further down the line, on the evening of 22 May, some claimed that the fort was once again wholly in French possession. In fact, confidence was so high that Mangin was able to pronounce, 'Douaumont is ours!' But it was not. The next morning, the 34th Division was thrown into the breach as reinforcement, with the order 'to advance upon the fort, occupy it, defend it at any cost against attack and clean out . . . any lingering Germans'.

But the attack now began to falter. Suitably reinforced from underground passages into the fort, the Germans mounted a fierce rearguard action. As a result, any French reinforcements, such as the 34th, were repelled as they attempted to enter the bulwark. An isolated group of

French infantry ensconced, yet effectively isolated on the western side of the fort, received instructions to continue with the attack. But they were severely depleted in able-bodied men, and no supporting formations could penetrate the intense German fire. The captain of the force voiced the concern that 'no one will come back alive'.

The situation for the French worsened throughout the day and culminated as a completely hopeless one. Cut off and encircled, the French troops inside the fort had ultimately to concede defeat and surrender. The loss was a heavy one. Countless infantry had been killed or wounded during the advance on the fort and, following the capitulation, about 1000 prisoners had been taken by the Germans. These were reverses on a scale that the beleaguered French line could ill afford. With seeming victory snatched away so quickly and so ruthlessly, morale, too, was shattered.

At an earlier phase of the Battle of Verdun, an anonymous officer of the III Corps had expressed the opinion that, 'I would rather do nothing than embark upon an operation which has been ill prepared'. But this latest campaign was neither well timed nor, from an infantry point of view, properly prepared. In view of the available manpower, it was perhaps more than a little premature. Characteristically, Pétain had warned prior to the attack that it should be postponed until sufficient numbers were available, and then carried out only on a wider front. But his opinion carried little weight, squeezed as it was between the equally impatient offensive tendencies of Joffre and Nivelle. One commentator thought the entire attack symbolized 'the dramatic, courageous futility that characterized the Battle of Verdun as a whole'. The casualty figures certainly support such a conclusion: some 900 dead, 2900 wounded, and 1600 'missing'. Thus, of the 12,000 or so French men mobilized for the mission, 5400 had been rendered inactive by the end of it. The total gains were nil.

In the usual manner of things, such a heavy loss would not be accepted lightly by the French General Staff, and another immediate onslaught was considered. But events took an unprecedented turn. Upon serious contemplation of the situation on the ground and the total French numbers available at Verdun, Mangin suggested that a follow-up attack should not be ordered. Perhaps taking a leaf out of Pétain's book, he thought it best to wait for the circumstances to change. He remained confident, nevertheless, that his time would come.

Following the raid on Fort Douaumont, conditions for the German garrison stationed there remained dreadful. The bulwark had been badly shaken and required some extensive repair works. Furthermore, it was se-

Fort Douaumont as it stands today

verely overcrowded, mostly with the wounded and unwell. The hitherto
highly efficient German medical operation was now beginning to struggle
with the amount of work required of it. It was estimated that, by the end
of May, medics were losing 40 per cent of all wounded soldiers in trying
to evacuate them from Fort Douaumont to a clearing hospital some 6
kilometres away.

For the French, confidence plummeted. The general morale of the
poilus had been adversely hit by another apparently futile exercise that had
seen their ranks annihilated. The ascendancy of Nivelle and Mangin had
done little to inspire further their overall belief in the cause which, now
more than ever, seemed a hopeless one. It was following this latest disaster
around Fort Douaumont that the first, small signs of indiscipline became
discernible through the line.

Conversely, for the Germans, the general outlook was now better than
it had been for some time. The French were clearly losing some heart and,
moreover, men and materials were once again flowing freely to the front
in support of the forthcoming German push across the right bank. In the
meantime, there was no let-up in the intensity of the war. One Frenchman noted:

. . . the violence of the battle is not wearing itself out; it rages more furiously than ever. Our feelings get beyond us; tormented by horror and distress, harrowed by passion and hatred, they either carry us away, or they rebel altogether.

In accordance with Knobelsdorf's wishes – and he was now the undoubted driving force behind offensive operations at Verdun – the Germans spent the last days of May concentrating efforts for a powerful attack on the right bank of the Meuse. The aim was now the relatively straightforward one of establishing a firm base from where the last, final push towards the city of Verdun could be launched. As ever, planning was meticulous. Circumstances – namely, the heavy casualty totals that were daily mounting – dictated that all pretence of tactical subtlety now be dropped. The Fifth Army intended to exploit what its command believed to be a numerical superiority in infantry and unquestionable superiority in artillery. Under the sheer weight of the attack – which would be comparable to the initial February onslaught – France's resistance, it was believed, would be shattered. Three infantry Corps, the I Bavarian, X Reserve, and XVth, would advance along the narrowest of fronts, barely 5 kilometres in width.

In response, the French could muster barely five divisions. From the beginning of June, all resources – munitions, men, even some rations – were being withheld in anticipation of the forthcoming Somme offensive. So, at the very point when the Verdun conflict reached an unprecedented intensity, the defending line was more stretched than ever. This did not bode well for the immediate future. On 31 May, Nivelle tried to rally his troops, telling them in an Order of the Day: 'We must have courage, men! We must not for a moment allow any weakness to endanger the outcome of so many heroic efforts.'

The Germans chose as the initial focus for the attack the fort at Vaux. Repeated attempts at capturing this ever-present flanking scourge of their right-bank infantry had, to date, all failed. For months, 420-mm artillery guns had rained down explosives on the position but it still held out. The renewed artillery bombardment proceeded on 1 June, featuring the usual mixture of heavy calibre shells, and introducing a deadly new weapon, phosgene – or green-cross – gas (an incredible 110,000 gas shells were used against the area around Fort Vaux in the first week of June alone). Thereafter, the infantry advanced upon the fort from a north-westerly direction, across ravines and shell-swept land and through a heavy flanking counter-barrage. The treacherous ground was covered bravely and in relatively quick time.

Fort Vaux was easily the second most important fortification

Fort Vaux

Strategically, Fort Vaux's importance was second only to that of Fort Douaumont in the Verdun region. It fulfilled an integral role during combat in the 1916 battle, and was the scene of one of the most stubborn and heroic defences seen anywhere during World War I.

The fort was located at the edge of the Meuse hills, overlooking the Woërve Plain, to the south-east of Fort Douaumont. Its position offered excellent observation opportunities, and allowed for its outward-facing guns to be aligned to work in conjunction with those at Fort Douaumont.

Begun in 1881, the position took three years to build and was reinforced immediately before 1914. Modestly armed, the fort was nevertheless a formidable concrete defensive position. It suffered from various logistical problems, however, such as poor ventilation and inadequate sanitary arrangements. This did not prevent French soldiers and reservists operating in front of Verdun from crowding into the position during the early years of the war. This reflected the reality that, before February 1916, Fort Vaux saw little action of note.

Under the scheme of fortification down-grading, in 1915 Vaux lost its fixed garrison of 250 men. A skeleton force – left to man the fort's two observation posts and 75-mm gun turret – was left *in situ* but was constantly being augmented by detachments in retreat from engagements on the slopes of the Meuse hills.

In the early days of the 1916 battle, Fort Vaux was subjected to a number of violent artillery attacks that all left their marks. In early March, the position's communication channels with command HQ were destroyed by enemy fire. Thereafter, the fort continued to function well short of its theoretical capability, though the lesson of the débâcle at Fort Douaumont had been learnt and the position was kept well armed.

With the capture of Fort Douaumont in late February, the fort at Vaux became the next major obstacle in the way of a German advance on Verdun. Consequently, it became the focus of much of the offensive efforts across the right bank. It has been estimated that, during March, April, and May, an estimated 8000 shells a day were directed towards Fort Vaux.

Yet the position held. It was only in the aftermath of a renewed push across the right bank that, in early June, German forces managed to violate Fort Vaux. Even then, they could not readily defeat the French garrison there. The ensuing siege for possession of the bulwark lasted five days and cost the Germans dearly. The defence – overseen by Major Raynal – was obstinate and effectual in equal measure, restricting German gains to a mere 65 metres. With no water supply and no support, however, Raynal's men could not be expected to prolong indefinitely their ferocious hand-to-hand rearguard. At six o'clock on the morning of 7 June, the position was surrendered.

The recapture of Fort Vaux became a major objective of the French counter-offensive launched in October 1916. The first attempt, on 25 October, failed despite a formidable artillery barrage being focused upon the position. Before a second effort could be launched, however, the shell-shocked German force withdrew from the fort, destroying its remaining functioning observation post. The French reclaimed the position on 2 November.

Despite all it had been subjected to, the fort at Vaux remained intact even though most of its military functions had been disabled. After retaking the position, the French set about restoring the fort's substantial defensive capability, which they employed until the end of the war.

Fort Vaux, scene of one of the most heroic defences of World War I

Two of Fort Vaux's gun emplacements

throughout the Verdun region, and was designed very much as the strategic twin of Fort Douaumont. Although only about a quarter of the size of the latter, Vaux stood some 8 kilometres from Verdun on the edge of the Meuse hills at an altitude of about 350 metres. It was an excellent observation post and its guns were set to work in tandem with Douaumont's. Begun in 1881, the fort took three years of intense effort to construct. Under a general scheme of fortifications' reinforcement before 1914, Fort Vaux was strengthened with an outer concrete casement 2.5 metres in width. Atop this was laid a further metre layer of sand.

During the early years of World War I, the fort was used mostly as a place for housing French detachments active in its vicinity. It saw little direct action before 1916 and was not utilized as a defensive position. It was seen as being something of a safe house, however, and consequently functioned as a magnet attracting front-line soldiers, reservists, and other military support workers who would retire there seeking replenishment and solace. Overcrowding was a perennial problem that a number of the fort's commanders tried and failed to overcome.

Fort Vaux was beset by similar logistical problems to those of its counterpart at Douaumont. There was no allowance for burying the dead nor was there anywhere, other than outside the structure, for disposing of debris and waste. There was no electricity – lighting was by candle or gas lamp – so that movement within the fort was extremely difficult during an artillery attack.

Most surprising of all, Fort Vaux's communications system was completely inadequate and, under the exigencies of the battle, hardly functioned at all. The fort's command was left in a state of almost continual isolation, and had to rely on flashlights and flares. Poor visibility meant that such methods did not always suffice. When this happened, carrier pigeons became the only means of communicating with the outside world. Furthermore, the fort's internal communications were of an extremely poor standard, and depended on look-outs observing the battle area, then reporting back to the commander what they had seen. The system did not always work well and was most cumbersome. During the first months of the Battle of Verdun, all but one of the fort's observation posts were destroyed by enemy fire.

Under Joffre's scheme of fortification downgrading in 1915, Vaux lost all but a few of its fixed garrison, and its one heavy gun was removed – there was no 155-mm piece, only a 75 mm – leaving the position with nothing stronger than shielding machine-gun encasements. In February 1916, an enemy shell completely destroyed the one 75-mm gun turret.

Like Fort Douaumont, at the time of the concerted attack on it, Fort Vaux was operating well short of its theoretical capability. Nevertheless, lessons had been learned since the débâcle of 25 February, and the position was at least prepared to the best of its current capabilities for the possibility of an attack. It now had a sufficient supply of guns and ammunition and, it was supposed, carried enough supplies to feed and water its recently ensconced fixed infantry garrison of two companies.

Fort Vaux continued to attract French soldiers to it like moths to a flame, however. At the time of the German offensive, it was crammed to the hilt with some 600 troops. The majority of these were wounded, most of them from the effects of the estimated 8000 shells a day that had been pouring down in the neighbourhood of the fortress since March. Consequently, the area had been relentlessly assailed by a storm of steel that claimed a steady harvest of victims. Now, under an even more concerted effort, there was no way in or out of the position. 'Amid an ocean of destruction', Blond has written, the fort 'was like a giant lifeboat, crowded with survivors, men wounded and lost or cut off from their units.'

Despite a frenetic French rearguard, the speed with which the German infantry managed to advance on the fort encouraged the commander of the XV Corps, General von Deimling, to bring forward the planned storming of the position. There was little preparation for deviating from the original plan – by which any advance into the structure of the fort itself was still a matter of days away – but the Fifth Army's command relented and, at 3 o'clock in the morning of 2 June, the infantry emerged from captured trench positions just ahead of the fort and descended upon the bulwark.

Fort Vaux's interior, where for five days in early June 1916, French and German troops engaged in deadly hand-to-hand combat

All that day, artillery pounded away as the respective infantries, across the battlefield, engaged in their usual mortal combat. The attacking force proceeded cautiously – under the prevailing conditions, it had little choice – and, by the evening, had overrun a number of important French entrenchments ahead of the fort. All the while, the fort's machine-gunners struggled to fend off the advancing infantry, subjected as they were to a torrent of enemy shell fire. They managed nevertheless to arrest the approaching force.

Shortly before dawn, the most forward attacking line had managed to penetrate as far as the fort's surrounding moat. Moving in simultaneously from north-easterly and north-westerly directions, some German infantrymen managed to clamber on to the top of the position. The 50th Division, to the north-east, were the first to achieve any tangible success. Before sunrise they had forced one of Vaux's main machine-gun posts to surrender, knocking out its crew and its weaponry and taking a number of

Sleeping quarters at Fort Vaux

prisoners. The progress of the 151st Division, to the north-west, was far more treacherous. Isolated and exposed all morning and for much of the afternoon, they bravely attacked another machine-gun detachment but, in this instance, resistance was far stiffer. Having failed to smoke out the large gallery's force with flame-throwers, the attackers made repeated attempts to bomb them into submission with grenades. The defence was prolonged and valiant but, one after the other, guns and men fell victim to the tenacity of the Germans. The position was finally overcome in the late afternoon.

With the fort's two most effective remaining weaponry positions knocked out, the pressure on the German line relented. It was now only a matter of time, or so it appeared, until the Germans made major inroads into the structure, especially following the discovery by the 151st of a major breach that had been covered over with sandbags. Their entry there forced a French evacuation from a major part of the upper fort.

By now, the French garrison inside Fort Vaux was under command to resist the invasion at all costs, and to fight until the bitter end, until all supplies and munitions were exhausted. Save from doing the unthinkable and surrendering, however, there was in reality little else that they could have done, cut off as they were from the rest of the French line. As the Germans attempted to penetrate the inner sanctums of the fort, the French were forced to fend them off every centimetre of the way and by whatever means necessary. Along the length of the fort's cramped and darkened passages, a pattern of deadly hand-to-hand combat was immediately established. It lasted for some five days, and was accompanied throughout by the reverberating din of 420-mm shells hammering away at the outside of the structure.

As time passed, the valiant defensive force found itself battling not only against the Germans but also against the ever-diminishing odds of survival. One of the first actions undertaken by the enemy was to fill in the fort's crude air-ventilation system, thereafter opening it only to pour gas into the bulwark. With oxygen scarce, breathing became a major problem for some. Then there was the constant booming of the artillery, enough to test the nerve of even the most stoic and battle hardened of men. Furthermore, the Germans unleashed within the confines of the fort every small weapon available to them – not just gas and hand-held guns but also flame-throwers and grenades. Hand-to-hand combat – with the French fighting from behind barricades made of sandbags – usually involved bayonets, spades, and other similar weapons. Communication with other French positions remained tenuous at best, and no one could be sure whether or not desperate pleas for help reached their intended destination.

Despite all this Fort Vaux held out. Ultimately, it was an oversight in preparation before the attack that finally forced a capitulation. The water supply had been gravely overestimated. Early on the second day of the siege it was discovered that the two reservoirs supplying the fort's enlarged garrison were running dangerously low. The very real problem of thirst was to bring about an ultimate surrender.

The commander of Fort Vaux was the 49-year-old Major Sylvian-Eugène Raynal. Wounded earlier in the war, he moved only with the aid of a walking stick. Raynal had been given control of the fort in late May because, in the wider order of things, it represented a supposedly easier life. It was he who pleaded for the relief that never came and oversaw the most stubborn defensive defiance seen anywhere at the Battle of Verdun. Pétain termed the resistance 'simply a matter of honour' but it was surely more than that which restricted the entire German advance over the five days to a mere 65 metres, and which inflicted nearly 2700 dead on the

R. P. - 307 bis. La Guerre 1914-18 (Visé Paris 307 bis)
Le FORT de VAUX (Meuse) dont l'héroïque défense par le commandant RAYNAL et
une poignée de braves fut une des plus sublimes de notre histoire
Vaux Fort Where one of the most Famous deeds Fook Place

Despite constant shelling by artillery, Fort Vaux – in common with its counterpart at Douaumont – was never rendered inoperable during the 1916 battle

enemy – not including some sixty-four officers – for a net loss of just twenty Frenchmen. Indeed, so resilient was the defence that, on one day, the Germans gained just 5 metres of ground.

A French second-lieutenant described the scene inside Fort Vaux that first week of June:

> Everywhere there was nothing but fire and dust . . . [The German] attacks were renewed every day, striking now at this point, now at that; never did we yield an inch of ground so long as there was a man to defend it. I will not speak . . . of all that we went through. No water, no revictualling; those who went out to bring us supplies never got back. The only thing that we were not short of was munitions. . . They attacked us from three sides at once, but they never got us in their claws . . .

Neither side had any choice other than to drag the dead to one side and leave them to decompose (earlier at Fort Vaux, the French had used chlorine of lime, stored as disinfectant, as an effective means of burning those corpses that could not be taken out for burial). Thus was the air inside the structure – already in short supply – absolutely poisonous and, with no latrines either, the stench became doubly worse causing many to collapse.

The first-aid post at Fort Vaux consisted of six wooden stretchers; by 7 June there were seventy-eight French wounded. This demonstrated that

Fort Vaux: 'If there is glory in war for the soldier, then he has won it here.'

the general defensive position was becoming ever less feasible. Thirst was the overriding concern of everyone, and it was driving the men insane. Some licked the fort's damp stone walls; others reverted to the practice of trying to imbibe their own urine. By the fifth day of the siege, Raynal could see:

> . . . my men broken with fatigue, silent and gloomy. If I had to call on them for still another effort, they would have been incapable of carrying it out. So I decided to serve out the last drops of the corpse-smelling water which remained in the cistern. It represented scarcely a quart per man; it was nauseous, it was muddy, and yet we drank this horrible liquid with avidity. But there was too little and our thirst continued . . .

Meanwhile, outside the fort the fighting was as intense as ever, and every day it seemed to the French inside Vaux as if the Germans increased the intensity of the artillery bombardment. Raynal thought, 'It was as if he [the enemy] guessed the drama which was being played out within' and noted that, in consequence, 'the sufferings of my men, above all of the wounded, increased terribly. Thirst, that horrible thirst raged.'

Throughout, Raynal continued to attempt to convey the full horrors of the situation within Fort Vaux to the rest of the French line. His repeated requests for reinforcements to be sent, or for a relieving attack, amounted to nothing. On 4 June he sent his last carrier pigeon out into the sky above Fort Vaux with a message. It read:

> We are still holding our position, but are being attacked by gases and smoke of very deadly character. We are in need of immediate relief. Put us into communication with [Fort] Souville at once for visual signalling. We get no answer from there to our calls.

At first, the bird would not fly into the gas-filled skies around Fort Vaux but was eventually coaxed out. Upon arriving at Verdun, it fell dead, having achieved its mission. Optical communications with defensive headquarters at Souville were established thereafter, and command headquarters sent the reply: 'Do not lose courage, we shall soon attack'.

Raynal waited all that night and the following day for an attack that never materialized. At nightfall on 5 June, he signalled the following desperate message to Fort Souville:

> I must be set free this evening, and must have supplies of water immediately. I am coming to the end of my strength. The troops, enlisted men and officers, have done their duty to the last, in every case.

The reply came: 'Do not lose heart!' But Raynal and his men did not have much more to give. Severely debilitated by thirst, they continued to fend off the attacking force but the task was becoming increasingly impossible to sustain under the circumstances.

All relief attacks were insufficiently mounted and, in the face of an entrenched and determined enemy, crumbled without getting very far. No supplies could be got to the fort as all its approaches were effectively cut off by the Germans. On the evening of 6 June, Raynal sent out his last message, only a part of which could be deciphered. It ran, '. . . you will intervene before we are completely exhausted. Vive la France!' Once more, no one was able to intervene positively on behalf of Raynal.

There was no option open to the Major other than to surrender. As he surveyed his force that last night, he noticed: 'My men, who drank no more, ate no more, slept no longer, only held themselves upright by a prodigy of will'. He could ask no more of them or of himself, and the next day, the white flag was flown from Fort Vaux.

It was another major loss for the French, of enormous strategic magnitude and consequence. As news of the surrender filtered back to command headquarters at Verdun, the order was given to activate the 'Line of Panic'. Reservists were sent out to start digging trenches on the very outskirts of the city of Verdun itself. Defeat seemed to have moved one giant step closer. Once again, alarm was the emotion pervading the French line.

Raynal and his men were taken prisoner. Despite ultimately achieving a victory, the Germans had been severely shaken by the strength and by the duration of the resistance at Fort Vaux. The Crown Prince thought it admirable, and said as much when he received Raynal at Stenay the day after the surrender. Affording the Major absolute courtesy in disregard of his status as a prisoner of war, he informed Raynal that he had been decorated with one of the highest orders of the *Légion d'Honneur*. He then presented an award of his own, returning to Raynal his previously confiscated sword.

The German force once more had a decisive victory within its grasp. On the left bank it had advanced beyond the Côte 304–Mort Homme–Cumières line, and the troops were pushing on to the villages of Avocourt to the west and Chattancourt further to the east. The situation on the right bank appeared to be even more promising. They had managed to overcome both the major fortresses in the area, knocking out in turn the biggest theoretical threats to their advancing line. They were now advancing on a number of important French-held positions and villages and pushing the defensive force back on to its last tenable point of resistance, the 'Line of Panic'. Now, the only major obstacle between the Germans and Verdun was the fort at Souville.

Heavy summer rain, however, was to hamper progress towards this position and, throughout the month of June, the daily mortality rate for both forces reached unprecedented levels. Following the capture of Fort Vaux – which French propagandists obviously attempted to play down – fighting became particularly intense around the village of Thiaumont, south-west of Fort Douaumont. This spot was strategically significant to the German advance on Verdun. As such, it now became central to offensive and to defensive operations on the right bank. After some initial German success, a spirited French rearguard forced a deadlock. Thereafter, for the next two months, the battle for the village ebbed and flowed in a deadly war of attrition that resulted in heavy losses for both sides.

The continuing defence of Verdun, which had so far shown only occasional signs of complete collapse, served to disguise the fact that morale was weakening among French forces, and discipline becoming a steadily worsening problem. In the aftermath of the capture of Fort Vaux, some

Fort Souville: the last major fortification between the Germans and Verdun

poilus began to question openly many of the situations their commanders were putting them into, and to ponder on the validity of some orders passed down the line. There were instances recorded of men refusing to return to trenches ahead of yet another apparently futile counter-move. In mid-June, rumours of an impending sit-down strike by the *poilus* started to filter back to the Verdun command.

In the immediate aftermath of the surrender at Fort Vaux, Nivelle was presented with an opportunity to underline to his army the imperative of carrying out to the letter all orders, and to continue the fight in accordance with prevailing military doctrine. On 7 June, at the height of the German offensive, the 291st Regiment surrendered to a man in the face of a horrific onslaught and the death of its commanding officer. This gave rise to a huge gap in the defensive line and left the 347th Division, fighting alongside the 291st, terribly exposed to the enemy and to the merciless fire of the German machine-gunners. Furthermore, the division was in a dangerously weak state. The head of one company, Second-Lieutenant Herduin, was fighting with only thirty-five fit men. About to be isolated from the rest of the line, he broke with tradition and ordered a tacit withdrawal. For no clearly discernible reason, however, other units of the 347th decided to partake in the retreat. Some men ran and did not stop until they reached the outer limits of the city of Verdun.

Nivelle chose to make an example of Herduin and a young Ensign by the name of Millaud. Without court martial, they were executed for cowardice by members of their own units. Nivelle then sent out an Order of the Day that stated: 'Do not surrender. Die on the spot rather than yield an inch.' The measures seemed to work, at least for the majority of the men, but nothing could reverse the doubts and scepticism felt by many. Matters were not helped by a general shortage of *materiel* – men, ammunition, even the artillery pieces in some cases were beginning to show signs of great wear. Thirst also became a problem of increasing severity. On the approaches to the battlefield a sign was posted which read, 'Road to the Slaughterhouse'. It was hastily removed but long remembered.

Many observers now recognized that the point had been reached whereby Verdun had to be held at all costs. If it collapsed, it was noted, the rest of the French Army elsewhere on the Western Front might quickly follow suit. Verdun had become a question of wider significance concerning morale – life and death, even – and it affected the whole of the nation. None other than Pétain recognized the importance of the situation. He wrote to Joffre on 11 June:

> . . . Verdun must not fall. The capture of this city would constitute for the Germans an inestimable success which would greatly raise their morale and correspondingly lower our own . . . [At] this moment [public] sentiment possesses an importance it would be inexpedient to disregard.

In the few days after the fall of Fort Vaux, the Germans were undoubtedly one decisive step away from Verdun, and as such, close to a triumph that was badly needed. But, yet again, at the vital moment they failed to grasp the initiative. Indeed, at the brink of total success, the advance began to falter.

Though no one knew it yet, critical events in other spheres of World War I combat were to have a deciding influence upon the battle that had raged at Verdun since February. The advantage was slowly to be turned irrevocably towards the French.

There was one reason why the German offensive ahead of Verdun started to waver in the second week of June when victory looked a formality. Falkenhayn was forced to transfer vitally needed units out of Verdun and to the Eastern Front, there to meet a serious new challenge mounted by the Russians. An all-out offensive along a front of some 320 kilometres was so successful that its architect, General Brusilov, was to have the attack named after him, the only World War I General to be honoured so. A brutal surge towards the Austro-Hungarian-held positions took the latter by complete surprise and, in the ensuing retreat, Germany's principle ally lost over half its fighting forces in the space of a week. It was only after German reinforcements arrived from all points on the Western Front – including seven divisions meant for Verdun – that the Russians were halted some 75 kilometres forward from their point of departure. Thereafter, Austria was all but broken as a fighting force, and had been saved from certain annihilation only by the intervention of Germany.

The real success of the campaign, however, was achieved in relieving the pressure on the French at Verdun – a primary aim of the offensive – and to draw vital German resources away from the Western Front at a critical time (the Somme offensive was only a matter of weeks away). Furthermore, the Romanians, who had been wavering about on which side they should enter the war, were persuaded to join the Entente Powers. In many respects, then, the war was everywhere taking a decisive turn against the Central Powers.

The Brusilov offensive was a calamity for the Germans and for the Austrians, and adversely effected the former's chance of success at Verdun. The disaster came about largely as an indirect result of Falkenhayn's secretive nature and his inability to get along with the Austrian Commander-in-Chief, Conrad (indeed, so poor were relations between the two that it was remarked at the time that they were like secret enemies). The German commander's decision not to inform his Austrian counterpart of the attack on Verdun before its launch in February angered Conrad for some time. But Falkenhayn was little concerned by the bad blood that existed between them. Falkenhayn believed that, militarily, Austria was comparatively weak and represented something of a liability as the Germans had occasionally to bolster its flagging forces at various locations.

Nevertheless, throughout the war Conrad remained determined that Austria should act in a manner befitting its 'Great Power' status. He was consequently determined that his forces alone should deal with the Russian menace. Therefore, he spent much of 1915 and 1916 concentrating on defeating lesser military nations in south-eastern Europe so that all his army's efforts could be concentrated against the prime foe along the Eastern Front. It was in pursuance of this goal that Conrad launched an offensive against the Italians thereby removing five of Austria's finest divisions from the Eastern Front. Crucially, Falkenhayn was not informed, probably from spite and in response to Conrad's earlier rebuff in February.

When the Russians attacked on 4 June, without warning and at Austria's weakest strategic point, collapse inevitably followed. Falkenhayn had no option other than to intervene in support of the crumbling Austrian line. In direct consequence, the offensive at Verdun was temporarily suspended, 'pending the liberation of additional forces'. The Crown Prince explained the interim phase of German strategy at Verdun in the following terms:

> The positions as held were to be fortified so as to economise men as much as possible, and our troops were to be echeloned in depth until such a time as further reinforcements and large supplies of Green Cross gas shell should be [made] available for use in another attack.

The situation was critical. The fact that the Germans were unable to sustain the offensive at Verdun at this time was indicative of just how overstretched, in the most general sense, their resources were. Just days away from the Somme offensive, German fortunes seemed to have taken a serious downward turn.

For the French the hiatus had come at a crucial time. They now had the opportunity to replenish the line and bulwark as best they could vulnerable defensive positions. Simultaneously, there would be no let-up in the counter-offensive. The artillery was kept rolling as a means of affording the 'resting' German forces no opportunity to do so. There could be no respite. The future of the French nation depended on Verdun remaining in French hands.

At this juncture, the Crown Prince made another attempt to persuade Falkenhayn to give up the attack on Verdun. The human costs remained intolerably high and, in the light of the wider picture that was evolving, constituted a continual waste of valuable resources. But, with the exhortations of the Kaiser and Knobelsdorf ringing in his ear, Falkenhayn would not countenance such a move. Too much had been committed at Verdun for the Germans simply to walk away now.

Despite being the man closest to the spot, once again the Crown Prince was not taken seriously by his military superiors nor his father. This was a problem that had beset his entire tenure as head of the Fifth Army. It was compounded by the fact that his troops tended to think of him as a bit of a joke. It was a problem of image. Simply put, the Crown Prince could not shake off his image. No one took much notice of his supposed 'personal sacrifice' at Verdun because he spent most of his days there at Stenay 40 kilometres or so from the front – this 'godforsaken hole' as he described it – playing tennis, riding, or carousing with one or other of his mistresses.

But this was unfair: it detracted from an earnest suggestion based on a rational analysis of the military and strategic situation as it stood. But no one listened to the Crown Prince and, as the moment of crisis passed for the French, the Germans remained obstinate in their designs on Verdun even though everywhere the tide had begun to turn against them.

Meanwhile, before the effects of Brusilov's action made themselves felt at Verdun, in a fleeting moment of deep pessimism, Pétain suggested that perhaps France's best hope of survival was to evacuate the right-bank positions thereby saving lives and valuable heavy weaponry. This, in turn, would allow the French the opportunity to establish more tenable lines of defence behind the city. General de Castlenau quietly but firmly dismissed the idea. Subsequent events were to show that he was right.

Nivelle's Order of the Day for 22 June read:

> This is the decisive moment. The Germans feel that they are being hunted down on all sides and are launching violent and desperate attacks against our front, in the hope of reaching the gates of Verdun before they are themselves attacked by the re-united forces of the Allied armies. Comrades, you must not let them pass.

Despite its obvious purpose as a means of bolstering troop morale, Nivelle's analysis of the situation was an incisive and realistic one. With each passing day, the French were gaining a little more of the initiative in combat. The attacking force ahead of Verdun was waning, being diverted as it was to other geographic locations of battle. The Germans' only realistic hope was to capture the city before the war elsewhere made such an advance unlikely. The Crown Prince now believed that there was 'no alternative but either to pursue the offensive with fresh forces or else abandon it for good'. The Somme offensive was about to deny the Germans the first option; and, with the Central Powers in retreat in the east, the latter would not be seriously considered. They had overcommitted themselves at Verdun, that much was understood, yet prestige and honour dictated no further withdrawals or capitulations in any sphere of operations.

On 22 June, the offensive towards Fort Souville was instituted once more. General Knobelsdorf took direct control of an operation that seemed as though it would make or break the German effort at Verdun. In the past ten days or so, the French had grasped the opportunity to fix as best they could the fort's battered defences – an estimated 38,000 shells had fallen on the position in the two months to 21 June – but, despite all their efforts, it remained in considerable disrepair.

The structure itself was comparatively small and, therefore, could not

French gas masks were crude and cumbersome, and often of
only limited use against phosgene

be compared directly with the forts at Douaumont and Vaux. Nevertheless, it occupied a strategically significant point in front of Verdun, and was of moderate combative strength. Souville was the last important obstacle before Verdun and, if the bulwark fell, it was almost certain that the city would follow, as it lay just a few kilometres *downhill* from the fort. The repercussions of the loss of Verdun – in a political and a military sense – would be severe, and no one could be sure whether the tottering French government could survive such a calamity. Consequently, the stakes were becoming ever higher.

Before the onslaught, Knobelsdorf was in confident mood and he felt certain his forces had what was needed to overcome Souville and wrest control of Verdun from the French. The mood among the rank and file had reached a nadir, however. Because it had been so long in the line and subject to the full brunt of the enemy's sniping infantry counter-attacks and artillery, the German infantry assembled for the attack was, in large part, tired of the battle and sick of the war. It required a prodigious mental effort to raise themselves for yet another colossal – but, it was widely felt, possibly futile – push on Verdun. As a mark of such feelings, the desertion rate had soared sharply throughout June.

Approximately 30,000 troops had been assembled for the offensive on Fort Souville. They would proceed along a concentrated front barely 5 kilometres across. On 22 June, an intense artillery bombardment 'softened' the area of attack all day. It lifted briefly in the early evening to make way for a hauntingly quiet shower of green cross gas shells. As the gas debilitated those units not already ravaged by the artillery fire, this prelude to the infantry thrust was devastating.

French gas masks were crude and cumbersome, and were of only limited use against the phosgene gas shells. Used by the Germans for the first time on such a scale, the weapon created chaos and panic as a smog descended upon, and hovered over, the French positions. The command was stumped for a response to the effects of this ghastly onslaught. The artillery positions were especially badly hit and, one by one, the right-bank batteries began to fall silent. Everywhere men collapsed and choked; ammunition mules buckled and died as the gas and the weight of their cargo weakened them. Doctors had no ready cure for the after-effects of the poison and could not be sure how to treat the victims. Some *poilus* attempted to light small fires as a means of staving off the deadly fog that had engulfed them.

At 5 o'clock on the morning of 23 June, the German infantry – feeling perhaps slightly more confident following the gas attack – began their advance, proceeding in dense formations with reserve lines tucked in tight behind the first line. For the best part of four hours, these lines were

The site of the village of Fleury. Between 23 June and 17 August 1916, Fleury changed hands some sixteen times

able to move virtually unhindered, and initial gains were good. In some cases, in an echo of the February attack, German troops walked across abandoned or obliterated French lines without even realizing the fact. By 9 o'clock, however, a stealthy infantry rearguard had been enacted by the French. Thereafter, the fighting was fierce, with each forward move being challenged. Every parcel of land was contested to the last. Around the village of Fleury, which changed hands some sixteen times between 23 June and 17 August and, not surprisingly, was obliterated as a result, the battle raged particularly hard. By the afternoon, it had fallen to the Germans, only to be recaptured by the French. By nightfall, however, it belonged again to the attacking force.

That evening, according to some reports, the German infantry force was barely 5 kilometres from Verdun; other witnesses claimed that wild German machine-gun fire reverberated through the abandoned streets of the city. No one could verify either assertion but Nivelle and his fellow commanding officers were unnerved enough to apply to the Commander-in-Chief for aid. For once, Joffre relented and immediately despatched to Verdun four divisions he had been holding back in anticipation of the Somme action.

They would arrive at the front just in time to witness the German offensive run out of steam. The French artillery counter-operations began to pay dividends in the early hours of 24 June. With the German front line ailing, reinforcement was desperately needed. The gunners suitably recovered from the gas attack, however, the French field guns had been working for some hours at full tilt and managed to prevent much-needed supplies of men and ammunition reaching their destination. At the same time, caution overtook Knobelsdorf who decided against launching another gas attack over the defending line.

Thirst was now beginning to get the better of many German units in the field. Tactically, the attack also started to pay the price of being overly concentrated. Although French infantry counters were being readily thwarted everywhere, the French artillery was achieving some notable successes against densely formed German positions. By late afternoon, Knobelsdorf had to concede that his bid to knock out Fort Souville had failed. French raids on the enemy continued throughout 25 June but resulted in no tangible gains. By the same token, neither did the German line move forward significantly. Needless to say, by the end of it, both sides were physically and mentally exhausted and, as ever, casualty figures were high.

On 1 July 1916, the long-planned and much-awaited Franco-British offensive along the Somme began. Coming so soon as it did in the wake of the Brusilov offensive, it represented for the Germans one challenge too many. They were now committed at a number of geographic locations and along two major fronts.

The infantry advance on the Somme followed seven days of continual artillery bombardment, and was brought forward by the British in accordance with French wishes to relieve some of the intense pressure on them at Verdun. The move succeeded in as much as, after this date, the German forces ahead of Verdun received no further divisional reinforcements. Those already in the line were left there, soon to be overtaken by crippling fatigue and a loss of all hope.

The intervention was crucial to the eventual denouement at Verdun. Not only were the German forces there pushed to the very limits of their endurance, and irrevocably weakened, the move also allowed Nivelle's men valuable time and space for regrouping. This proved essential as the process of reversing the tactical state of play around Verdun was enacted.

The pressure under which the French had for so long been operating now lifted considerably and, as July came, switched to the Germans. The Crown Prince was later to recall: 'We . . . entered upon the month of July with the intention of resuming the offensive, while yet we were compelled to devote all our energies repelling hostile attacks of the most determined kind'. The worsening wider picture adversely effected the already poor morale among all ranks of the German force, and was compounded by the unrelenting French barrage. Further, as well as the lack of fresh reinforcements, the Somme offensive led to a number of high-calibre artillery pieces being transferred from the Verdun region to Picardy.

Lacking troops and with a weakened arsenal, the Germans prepared for one final effort to break through to Verdun. The portents were not good but, nevertheless, three divisions were made ready to go into battle once more. On 9 July, the artillery opened up; the following day the infantry advanced again in the general direction of Fort Souville. The green cross gas had not proved to be as effective this time – the French were better equipped with improved gas masks to deal with it – and so it was that two evenly matched forces engaged each another. The two infantries contested bravely but the French artillery succeeded in blowing huge holes in the advancing German line.

The *poilus* took advantage of this and gradually gained the upper hand. Nevertheless, they were powerless to halt a brave and fearsome drive that saw thirty men of the German 140th Regiment reach Fort Souville on 12 July. From its roof, the Germans – the only ones to do so from the battlefield during the Verdun campaign in 1916 – glimpsed briefly the spires of the city's cathedral and momentarily flew a German ensign from the top of the structure. But they were soon repelled from within the fort by a small-scale, but highly effective, French counter-operation. Like Vaux before it, Fort Souville had withstood the most ferocious efforts of the enemy artillery. Outwardly, it may have been battered beyond recognition but it still stood. As one French commentator observed after the war, the *poilus*, through their dogged determination, may have done most to thwart the Germans before Verdun, 'but concrete contributed its share'.

Thereafter, the exhausted, beleaguered German infantry was pushed back. On the evening of 11 July, the Crown Prince had already received the following instruction from German general headquarters: 'as the objectives of today's attack have not been reached . . . the Crown Prince's Group of Armies will henceforward adopt a defensive attitude'. It was over. The high point of the German advance had passed. The advantage was now firmly with the French.

9

End Game

> You say that you will soon hold Verdun,
> whilst really Verdun holds you.
>
> from a French
> 'trench' newspaper

AS SOON AS the general strategic situation before Verdun became evident, military men, politicians, and the French public alike began to clamour for a forceful offensive immediately to be instituted to expel the Germans from the Verdun sector. But, as the relative ease with which the Germans repelled its earliest counter-strokes readily testified, the French force was clearly not yet prepared for such a strenuous undertaking. Indeed, for the rest of July and much of August, the battle sustained itself in the expected, bloody fashion with artillery and infantry on both sides combining to ensure that the tragic slaughter continued.

Occasional instances of panic continued to take hold in the French line as they struggled to contain the German positions on both banks of the Meuse. The French suffered greatly from the fact that they could never be completely certain that the Germans had, in reality, completely abandoned all designs on taking Verdun. The fear lingered that, at any day, the offensive might be resumed. Furthermore, a determination persisted not to allow the Germans off the hook, and this kept French minds focused. Nivelle told his men:

> . . . soldiers of the Second Army, you must not be content with resistance.
> By continued and incessant pressure on the enemy, you must force him to
> keep in line against you as many of his troops as you can hold there, until
> the hour strikes, as it soon will, for the general offensive.

In fact, the Germans were playing a similar tactical game, keeping the French fully engaged at Verdun so that they were unable to release extra reinforcements to the Somme region. All the time, though, their gains on the left and the right banks were becoming increasingly vulnerable and, it was realised, daily more exposed to the likelihood of a ferocious counter-

The Generals Hindenburg and Ludendorff, who assumed joint
control of German operations along the Western Front following
the removal of Falkenhayn to the Romanian front

attack. At no time was a withdrawal considered, however. The need to
maintain honour remained, and it was recognized that the psychological
impact of any such move would be profoundly felt throughout the rest of
the German Army. In any case, as Falkenhayn informed the Crown
Prince on 21 August, it was 'urgently necessary to keep the enemy in the
Meuse area under the impression that the offensive on the German side
has not been abandoned but will be systematically continued'.

In this, at least, they succeeded, while continuing to contest every centimetre of ground that became the object of a French counter-move. Despite
the lingering appearance of an offensive stance, however, by late August the
Germans had started to wind down all operations in the Verdun sector, and
most activities came to an almost complete standstill. Arguably, it had by
now become easier for the Germans to move backwards.

Knobelsdorf, recently the main exponent of the offensive before Verdun, had already been transferred to operations in Russia. The Crown Prince had long since abandoned any hopes of glory and completely lost interest in the entire, calamitous affair. Falkenhayn, meanwhile, paid the price for the failure of his grand plan, and his resignation was accepted by the Kaiser in late August. He was transferred to operations against Romania – where he enjoyed some success – and was replaced in the west by the Generals Hindenburg and Ludendorff.

In the end, the German High Command settled on the calculation that, at Verdun, they were paying too high a price for a prize that ultimately was probably not worth the effort. Further, it was seen clearly that the French were not suffering nearly enough, and certainly, were not being bled into total submission. Moreover, morale was at an all-time low, worsened by poor weather and problems of supply. It was only a matter of reputation that kept the line where it was.

As it became clear that Verdun was no longer under any serious or immediate threat, confidence rose among the French. All efforts were now concentrated on preparing for a far-reaching counter-stroke to try to regain all land that had been lost since February. In early September, Mangin uncharacteristically agreed to desist from minor skirmishes and localized counter-attacks in favour of conserving energy and resources for the bigger push. Consequently, for the first time in some seven months, relative quiet descended over the scarred hills and ravines to the north of the city of Verdun.

There was, however, one more disaster yet to befall the French force at Verdun. On 4 September, the single-track railway tunnel at Tavannes, south of Fort Vaux, caught fire killing some 500 troops who were camped inside it. It was a shocking and avoidable accident, started when a munitions dump caught fire sparking a rapid chain reaction.

Throughout the battle the tunnel had been used by French units as a shelter. It was obviously unsuited to the task but, nevertheless, sufficed under battle conditions that offered no cover for days on end. Therefore, the tunnel was perpetually overcrowded with front-line troops and reservists together with their weapons, ammunition, and horses. There was no adequate lighting, poor ventilation, and no sanitary arrangements other than a ditch that ran the length of the tunnel which was never cleaned for fear of releasing some dreadful disease. Jacques Meyer called the tunnel purgatory, a seemingly apt description.

When the explosion occurred, it was followed rapidly by fireballs that burnt to a cinder everything in their path. Some of those men closest to the tunnel's entrance tried to escape but were mown down by enemy

The railway tunnel at Tavannes, where some 500 French troops lost their lives following a mass explosion on 4 September 1916

machine-gun fire. The inferno took three days to burn itself out. There was only a handful of survivors.

Since it had fallen on 25 February, Fort Douaumont had become the symbol of progress for both the armies engaged at Verdun. There were some hard-line optimists on the German side who still felt that, as long as their forces continued to hold the bulwark, there was still hope. But, in view of the general lie of the land following the suspension of all offensive manoeuvres, this amounted to no more than a fantasy. For the French, on the other hand, there would be no rest until Douaumont and Fort Vaux were retaken.

It was to this end that French offensive planning was aimed. For perhaps the first time since the earliest stages of the battle, the French command was united in its commitment to the means by which to achieve a military end. Nivelle, Mangin, and Pétain oversaw preparations for an offensive which, in its precision, came close to the German arrangements before the February onslaught.

The scale of the operation was quite unprecedented. Previously at

Verdun, the French command had worked mostly on an *ad hoc* basis, reacting to events rather than controlling them. Now, for the first time, they had the opportunity properly to orchestrate their actions in advance. Consequently, there was always a far greater chance that the outcome would resemble their original intentions. Now, Pétain's tactical thinking was to come to the fore; the infantry would advance in a piecemeal fashion but only after superiority on the ground had first been guaranteed by an artillery bombardment. The *poilus* were assured that there was to be no wasteful and unnecessary human slaughter. Any sacrifices would be an inevitable consequence of enemy counter-moves and an unfortunate necessity if France were to be victorious at Verdun. But no one would die in vain.

Pétain ensured the requisition and assembly of all the necessary artillery pieces and ammunition. Some 650 cannons were amassed, over half of them of heavy calibre. A number of 370-mm naval guns were made available for the operation, and two brand-new 400-mm weapons arrived at Verdun. The French had seen nothing like it before in the sector. To supplement these batteries, throughout September, ammunition began to arrive in bulk, until tens of thousands of tons of shells had been stockpiled. It was all camouflaged and stored, ready for the assault.

Infantry preparations were mostly Nivelle's domain. Three divisions, all with specific remits, were assembled and drilled ahead of the advance. The 38th Division under General Guyot de Salins was to be used against Fort Douaumont; the 133rd Division, led by *La Gauloise*, General Passaga, would proceed in the gap between Douaumont and Fort Vaux; and against Vaux would go the 74th Division, under the command of General Lardemille. These were all to pursue a new technique of attack, masterminded by Nivelle and known as the 'creeping barrage'. Simply put, this allowed for infantry and artillery to work more closely in tandem with the latter pinning back the enemy, allowing the former to advance over shell-swept land largely unhindered by any oncoming fire. It represented a fine tuning of existing battle methods but, crucially, required immaculate timing, communications, and pre-planning. The three divisions and artillery batteries were given exhaustive training, and further, the *poilus* were put through their paces in September near Bar-le-Duc where a mock-up of the Fort Douaumont battle area allowed them to rehearse the actual operation.

The German line grew increasingly uneasy for they could guess what lay ahead of them and there was little they could do about it. Confidence among the infantry was not improved by the impression that the Fifth Army's command had completely given up on Verdun and was no longer pressing for much-needed reinforcements. Consequently, those unlucky

A French shell factory

enough still to be at Verdun at this late stage – and plenty, such as the VII Reserve Corps, had been there from the start – were apparently being abandoned to their fate. There was a desperate shortage of men and no hope of replenishment; most big guns were worn out and no longer up to the job. It was a near reversal of the situation at the start of the year: the French were confident – de Salins told his men, 'your victory is certain' – and up to strength while the Germans were harassed and lacking in resources. The desertion rate among German troops remained high throughout late summer and early autumn. Some defected because it was the only way to escape the steady stream of French shells, fired to ensure that vital bulwarking work was not carried out on depleted defences. In *Education Before Verdun*, Arnold Zweig described the condition of German soldiers at this time:

> The Germans had held on hitherto beyond all imagination . . . [reduced now to] about seventy thousand men, scattered and lost in that ravaged land. They had starved, they had crouched waist-high in watery slime, they had burrowed into the mud because it was their only cover, they had not slept, they had struggled against fever and held on. And now they were be-ginning to crack.

The French force fell into line on 19 October shortly before the artillery began its attack. It was a freezing-cold day and heavy rain had turned the battle zone into a quagmire. Captain Gillet described the terrain in the vicinity of Fort Douaumont as:

> this diluted clay, greasy as butter . . . so much stirred and lashed by shells that it has become a great efflorescence of scum, with the consistency of soap lather and that appearance of a vast surface of boiling milk which characterises a raging sea.

Overhead, observation aircraft witnessed the initial artillery barrage make a number of accurate hits. The new 400-mm pieces aimed shells directly on to Fort Douaumont. Some observation posts and gun encasements were obliterated. Over the next few days, the bombardment was unrelenting. Panic began to spread among the fort's garrison. Munitions stores were hit, and a series of fires spread throughout the infrastructure. Meanwhile, the water supply was running out. It seemed as though a deadly disaster was about to engulf the holding force. The fort's commander, Major Rosendahl, was increasingly powerless to hold his men in line. He therefore ordered the evacuation of the top of the fort's structure. The process was mostly completed during the late evening of 23 October.

After some four days in position, the French infantry emerged from wet shell holes and muddy trenches and advanced upon a largely abandoned Fort Douaumont. Their approach to the fort was rapid and precise, with the 'creeping-barrage' technique working well. Communication between infantry and artillery positions remained good – to guarantee this, telephone lines had been dug to what was thought to be the safe depth of 6 feet – so the operation ran relatively smoothly. German trenches had been mostly destroyed, and the general enemy response was negligible. Many surrendered without putting up a struggle though a few were determined to fight to the bitter end.

Those Germans still lingering within the structure of the fort had virtually no capacity for fighting. They had neither the ammunition nor the strength to try to thwart the advancing enemy. Consequently, the French were able to retake the fort at Douaumont with similar ease to the German capture of it some eight months before. One bitter scuffle erupted during 25 October when a small pocket of fewer than 30 German infantrymen, led by a Captain Prollius, re-occupied a part of the position, determined to defend it to the hilt. But they were overpowered in the end, and the fort was finally reclaimed in a matter of hours.

The French were jubilant and amazed to discover that, despite months of being subjected to some of the heaviest and most constant shelling seen

The infantry on both sides became demoralised by the intensity of fighting and long duration of the Battle of Verdun

anywhere before Verdun, the infrastructure's interior remained in remarkably good order. Conversely, the loss was a symbolic one for the Germans. They had suffered heavy casualties but offered weak resistance. In the drive on Douaumont, they had been pushed back relentlessly. The village of Fleury fell for the last time, back into French hands. The *Daily Telegraph* war correspondent, E. Ashmead-Bartlett, thought Fleury to be 'the high-water mark of [German] success at Verdun gained at the most costly price paid by any nation for a worthless conquest'. Certainly, the eventual ease with which the remains of the village were lost seemed to characterize the fatuity of the lingering German presence in front of Verdun.

Any German counter-moves were now feeble and easily repelled, although machine-gunners continued to cause some casualties among the French infantry. In the face of a determined French advance, however, the ground gained at so high a price since February began steadily to slip away. The French were unforgiving in the sheer force with which they pursued their erstwhile tormentors. The infantry gave no quarter at any position, and the artillery continued to hammer away at the opposing line.

At Fort Vaux, French 370-mm and 400-mm shells were falling so torrentially that, in early November, the position was evacuated, with the retreating Germans demolishing part of the structure. With its defensive and strategic functions now almost non-existent, the fort represented little more than a symbol of national pride for the French. The Second Army re-occupied it, amid muted rejoicing, on 2 November.

Yet, even now, with all major gains lost and territory being rapidly conceded everywhere, the Germans remained determined to uphold their prestige and to continue the fight. As a result, long-range artillery fire was directed at Forts Douaumont and Vaux to ensure that the French could not rest for a moment nor turn the forts' guns upon the retreating line. Because of the difficulty of arming and supplying the fortresses, therefore, their guns lay mostly silent for the rest of the battle. Heavy fighting continued around the positions for some weeks to come, however. Ashmead-Bartlett observed the consequences:

French trenches had continuously been cut through this ground and in many places you found the dead embedded in the walls of trenches, head, legs, and half-bodies just as they had been shuffled out of the way by the picks and shovels of the working parties. It was a ghastly sight.

Here lay some of the best of a generation of two nations – sons and brothers, husbands and lovers – unidentified in the freezing earth of a muddy battlefield.

By December 1916, the tide of events in all spheres of the war had turned dangerously against the Central Powers. On 12 December the German Chancellor, Bethmann-Hollweg, offered to open peace negotiations with the Entente countries, in a neutral country and with President Wilson of the United States perhaps serving as mediator.

But the allies were not done yet and, at Verdun, neither were the French. Three days after Bethmann-Hollweg's proposals were tabled, the final, major offensive against the Germans was instigated. It was a year to the day since Falkenhayn had penned his memorandum to the Kaiser. The French plan was to push the enemy beyond where it had come from in February. Once more, planning was thorough, and the forces arrayed formidable. Four divisions proceeded to the north of Fort Douaumont: Guyot de Salin's 38th; General Muteau's 126th; Passaga's 133rd; and, under General Garnier-Duplessis, the 37th Division. Second-line reinforcements, if required, would be provided by another four primed

Such was the intensity of artillery shelling that, at Verdun, trenches were often obliterated

German prisoners of war at Verdun

divisions. The total artillery force, meanwhile, had been enlarged to 740 pieces.

Everywhere the French line – now more determined than ever – pushed back the utterly demoralized enemy force which, by this stage, could offer hardly any resistance. Between 24 October and the end of the year, the French took an amazing 60,000 prisoners-of-war in the Verdun sector as well as sixty-six heavy guns. Their advance was irresistible, the defence negligible. When the French came to a halt, what remained of the German force stood 3.5 kilometres to the north of Douaumont, some 6.5 kilometres from its most advanced point at Verdun.

The counter-moves had been emphatic. On 24 October alone, General Mangin had recovered as much terrain as it had taken the Germans four-and-a-half months to capture. As Basil Liddell-Hart was to observe, the General had retaken 'by bites what had been lost by nibbles'. The Crown Prince was powerless to prevent the loss of 'the blood soaked ground we had so dearly won'.

Verdun was safe. In a moment of absolute triumphalism, the French President, Raymond Poincaré, in bestowing upon the city the *Légion d'Honneur*, announced to the world that it was upon the walls of Verdun that 'the supreme hopes of Imperial Germany was crushed'. It was a statement imbued with more than just a grain of truth.

The Battle of Verdun was over. Occasional fighting around the environs of the city continued sporadically throughout the remainder of the war

The Trench of Bayonets

It can be of little surprise that, in the aftermath of World War I, the Battle of Verdun became enshrouded in many myths that held great currency. The battle's very length and brutality, as well as the many instances of heroic resistance shown in the face of adverse odds, aided the development and retelling of stories that were based only partly upon sustainable fact.

One of the most enduring Verdun legends concerns the 3rd Company of the 137th French Infantry Regiment. Occupying a trench, Ravine de la Dame, on the right bank until 11 June, the Company was exposed to the most ferocious infantry and artillery fire. By the next day, the unit had completely disappeared, to no one's great surprise it would seem, for its place in the line was subsequently filled with little fuss.

After the war, the trench – which had been filled – was discovered with a line of bayonets protruding from the earth. Upon excavation, the site

The Trench of Bayonets . . .

was discovered to be the burial place of the remnants of 3rd Company. The story quickly spread that rather than give way to the enemy, the men of the 3rd had chosen instead to be buried alive, to die on the spot rather than concede their position. The advancing Germans thereafter left the bayonets where they were, in lieu of wooden crosses.

Whether this was actually the way in which the 3rd Company died is a moot point. It certainly stretches credibility to the limit to suggest that the entire Company subscribed to some sort of predetermined suicide pact. It is more likely that they were taken unawares by the enemy's fire and instantly met an horrific death.

Either way, the mass grave caught the imagination of the French nation. In the early 1920s, a wealthy American, upon hearing the story, paid for a lasting concrete monument to be built on the site of the trench. It survives to this day, a symbol that celebrates the courage of the *poilus* who defended Verdun.

and as it has been preserved; a lasting monument to the defenders of Verdun

on the Western Front, but nothing to compare with the intensity of the engagement that had raged there for most of 1916. A few French trenches on the right bank were overrun during a German attack in June 1917 but the allies were not overly concerned. An offensive led by General Guillamat in August that year – in line with Nivelle's by now generally followed principle of attacking for limited gains – saw the recapture of the left-bank positions around Mort Homme and Côte 304. The entire operation took just four days, in stark contrast to the earlier battle for possession of the hill in the spring of the previous year.

The Verdun sector was finally cleared of German units in the autumn of 1918 as part of the general mopping-up process along the Western Front. A joint American-French operation, led by General Pershing, resulted in the Germans – outnumbered on the ground by three to one – being pushed back into the salient of St Mihiel.

There were, however, high-profile French casualties of the Verdun episode. In December 1916, Joffre was ousted as France's Commander-in-Chief. Increasingly unpopular and no longer trusted in political circles, his reputation – for so long bolstered by the success of the Marne – was all but shattered by the costly failure of the 1915 offensives. Furthermore, his actions before the attack on Verdun were not well regarded. The general down-grading of all fortresses, coupled with his lack of preparation prior to Verdun, were seen to have cost the French tens of thousands of lives. The failure of the Somme initiative – in which he had invested so much hope – added to the prevailing notions that Joffre was simply not up to the job of winning the war for France. Consequently, towards the end of the year, he was 'promoted' – like Pétain before him – to a supposed position of greater responsibility. He was accorded the title Marshal of France, and thereafter, played a wholly ceremonial role in the war, acting as a kind of roving ambassador for the allied war effort.

The obvious, and easily most popular, choice to replace him was Pétain. But he now paid the price for previously alienating too many men of influence, and was passed over. So it was Nivelle – basking in the glory of Verdun – who acceded to the posts of Commander-in-Chief of the French Army and Supreme Commander of the Allied Forces on the Western Front. General Guillamat, in turn, moved to the head of the Second Army. Mangin took over control of the Sixth Army.

With Nivelle overseeing all operations, the French pursued the rest of the war with an aggressive attitude, emphasis on the 'creeping barrage', greater flexibility of movement on the battlefield, and attempts at stemming casualty figures. Nivelle's reign at the top was short lived, however and, following the 1917 Spring Offensive, marred in bloody controversy. He professed to have the key to expedite the end of the war by employing on a mass scale the methods he had instituted so successfully at Verdun in the autumn of 1916 (Nivelle never tired of repeating the slogan 'We have the formula'). But the techniques did not transfer so well and, furthermore, the enemy had learnt a valuable strategic lesson and chose to defend in depth. Consequently, Nivelle's theories went up in smoke, as did the French infantry at Chemin des Dames. The result was a catastrophic rout and the shedding of yet more French blood. Ultimately, Nivelle was made to give way to Pétain.

There can be no doubt that the Battle of Verdun marked a watershed for the German and for the French army and that, after it, neither was the same in spirit and strength. For the Germans, Verdun was one episode in a fatal pantheon of occurrences that unfurled in 1916 that conspired to ensure that any realistic chance they had of winning the war all but seeped away. Some of their best units had been ruined before Verdun, and these could not be readily replaced. Fleeting success had been bought at high cost and with a much longer-term strategic consequence. After Verdun, people as diverse in their outlooks at Bethmann-Hollweg and Falkenhayn, came to believe that ultimate victory was beyond the Central Powers.

For the French, their mental and physical capacities had been through a mill of death and destruction, and the psychological scars this wrought took some time with which to come to terms. Most contemporary observers believed that nothing of the sort had been seen before, nor should it be again. Henry Bordeaux suggested that, 'At no spot on earth's surface has human courage in the face of suffering and death been more strikingly revealed'. The experience was to have serious repercussions for the continuing allied war effort. Thereafter, France's partners – especially Britain – would have to bear ever more of the burden of the war in the west. The French were simply not capable of mounting quickly such a monumental effort in the foreseeable future, and certainly not before the war was over.

Without question, the *poilus* could never again sustain such hardships or indignities. The after-effects of the Verdun experience undoubtedly sowed the seeds of mutiny which broke out in the ranks of the French Army in the aftermath of the calamity of Nivelle's offensive plans in May 1917. Provoked by a repeat of the kind of slaughter first experienced at Verdun, acts of so-called 'collective indiscipline' spread to some 20,000 men. Pétain blamed the disorders on pacifist propaganda emanating from Paris; de Gaulle later called the episode a 'disease', symptomatic of 'overstrain'. It was certainly more than a little coincidental that the mutiny erupted among those divisions who had spent longest in the line at Verdun. But, such a connection was officially denied at the time though its logic is certain.

10

The Balance Sheet

> Neither side 'won' at Verdun. It was
> the indecisive battle in an indecisive
> war; the unnecessary battle in an
> unnecessary war; the battle that had no
> victors in a war that had no victors.
>
> Alistair Horne, *The Price of Glory*

IN THE TEN months to December 1916, the French and German armies used an estimated 10,000,000 artillery shells against one another at Verdun. Some 1,350,000 tons of steel were dropped on the narrow battle zone north of the city. Total casualty figures for the battle are contentious but it seems fair to suggest that French losses, including the 'missing', topped 378,000; German casualties were in the region of 337,000. Nine villages had been forever erased from the map. And for what?

There can be little doubt that, at the Battle of Verdun, the least amount was gained at the highest of costs. At the end of the campaign neither side found itself any better off strategically. Indeed, the truth was that, in December 1916, following the success of the French autumnal counter-offensive, the Germans found themselves positioned barely a few hundred metres in advance of their initial February departure point. One contemporary commentator suggested that the Battle of Verdun represented 'one of the most serious checks received by the Germans' anywhere throughout the course of the war. He went on to note:

> [The German] High Command had foreseen neither [the battle's] amplitude nor its long duration . . . [T]he Germans found themselves in a formidable struggle, without being able either to obtain a decisive advantage or keep the relatively small advantages obtained at the beginning of the battle.

Falkenhayn's strategy at Verdun has been labelled a prime example 'of the folly of half measures'. Certainly, he had chosen to act in blatant disregard of German pre-war strategic thinking which asserted that, if it was to

The wounded lion monument which marks the point of the furthest German advance on Verdun

succeed, any attack on Verdun needed to be carried out on the broadest of fronts, that is, on both banks of the Meuse approaching the city. Furthermore, it was recognized that ample resources would be needed if Verdun was to be carried successfully.

Falkenhayn thought otherwise. He argued in retrospect that 'the lie of the land' on the left bank was not favourable to a wide-ranging attack. Instead, he chose to rely 'on a big initial success for our powerful thrust' across the right bank. When this failed to materialize, the Germans paid a heavy price for concentrating their attack on so confined a space, and they became increasingly hampered by flanking French attacks mostly from the left-bank positions around Mort Homme and on the right bank from Fort Vaux. Consequently, the High Command was forced to expand the frontage of the attack in any case.

If such a course of action had been instigated from the beginning – Falkenhayn's geographical considerations notwithstanding – there was a good chance that the French, unprepared as they were, would ultimately have been taken unawares and critically overwhelmed. Some years after the event, the Crown Prince alluded to the probable reasons for Falkenhayn's unwillingness to agree to this manner of undertaking, when he wrote:

> The limitation of the offensive to the right bank of the Meuse seemed to be motivated by a desire to engage as few troops as possible in the first stages, so as to ensure a continuous feeding of the front of attack over a longer period of fighting.

Other factors show that Falkenhayn's prime concern was anything but the rapid sack of Verdun. Foremost, there existed no need to take the offensive along the Western Front. The Germans had dug themselves in everywhere most effectively, and were managing successfully to repel all enemy incursions upon their line. If they were to attack in 1916, surely an offensive on another front against weaker opposition and at a less treacherous location would be more likely to succeed. Winston Churchill, in *The World Crisis*, thought Russia a likely target:

> One-half the effort, one-quarter the sacrifice, lavished vainly in the attack on Verdun would have overcome the difficulty of the defective communications in 'the rich lands of the Ukraine'. The Russian armies in the south would have been routed long before they had gained their surprising victories under Brusiloff [*sic*]; and Roumania [*sic*] . . . would have been brought into the war early not late and as an ally and not as a foe. But the school of formula had vanquished the school of fact, the professional bent of mind had overridden the practical; submission to theory had replaced the quest for reality. *Attack the strongest at his strongest point, not the weakest at his weakest point, was once again proclaimed the guiding maxim of German military policy.* [italics added]

So, rather than exploit the strategic weakness of one foe, Russia, Falkenhayn instead chose to gamble heavily on the likelihood of another, France, succumbing to a brutally unprecedented attack which was by no means guaranteed to yield the desired gains.

Yet, as Falkenhayn conceived the offensive it did have some merits. At the very least, the capture of Verdun would do little to weaken the German position on the Western Front because a tenuous protrusion into their line would be eradicated once and for all. Then there were the psychological consequences for France of such a loss to be considered; would the French be able to absorb such a reverse and continue their war effort unabated? Falkenhayn thought not, and he might have been correct in his thinking. So, regardless of whether his 'bleeding' experiment worked – and he saw no viable reason why it should not – the Germans had everything to gain and seemingly nothing of consequence to lose. But there was an oversight in the plan, inasmuch as there was always some chance that the Germans would 'bleed' in proportion commensurate to the French, especially once the latter were fully committed to defending the position to the last. This is what happened. From that point on, Falkenhayn's primary goal ahead of Verdun had been scuppered. It then became imperative that the city itself was taken.

In the end, the Germans succeeded in neither aim. This was because of a number of factors but, primarily, when it came to it they could not muster the necessary strength to overcome the French forces they had drawn into the defence of Verdun. The situation worsened with time as the requirements of operations elsewhere put additional strain on the overstretched German Army. Churchill commented that, 'The strategic and psychological conceptions which had led Falkenhayn to select Verdun as the point of the German attack became mingled in the tactical sphere'. As a result, when German losses became equal to those of the French, the fact was not recognized. No withdrawal was instigated, because the High Command failed to realize quickly enough that their strategy of attrition was costing them as much as it was the French. As Hindenburg was to comment later, 'This battle exhausted our forces like a wound that will not heal'. Ludendorff believed that the attack should have been terminated 'immediately it assumed the character of a battle of attrition. The gain no longer justified the losses.' More recently, a German historian has surmised that the strategy before Verdun:

> was too dogmatic, mechanical and rigid. Millions of men were thrown into the 'Meuse mill' in the hope that somehow the Germans would have the last men left standing. Or that the enemy would suffer moral collapse. Casualty lists took the place of surprise, deception, concentration, and manoeuvre.

The wider implications for the rest of the war were severe. The Germans were unable to recover substantially from the loss of personnel inflicted at Verdun. Moreover, the failure to break through had an adverse effect on morale. As the Crown Prince noted, Verdun 'ground up the hearts of the soldiers as much as their bodies'. Thereafter, a lack of faith in the High Command was widespread among the rank-and-file of the army, and discipline, hitherto so much a feature of the German military, slowly started to crack.

In terms of munitions, the Verdun offensive, coupled with the rearguard required on the Somme, stretched the efficient German war machine to its limit. All armament reserves were expended, forcing

Hindenburg to introduce, in August 1916, a programme that aimed to double munitions' output and to triple the production of machine-guns and artillery pieces by the spring of 1917. But the Ruhr industrialists were never able to catch up with demand, and the war effort remained critically destabilized.

The galling thing for many – foremost among them the Crown Prince – was that, in pursual of his 'bleeding' experiment, Falkenhayn passed over on a number of occasions the opportunity to exploit French defensive frailties and advance successfully on Verdun. At the end of February and twice during June, at the crucial moment, reservists were denied to the Fifth Army's command. On each occasion, a critical pause in operations let the French back into the battle. The failure to break through in June – when even the French command recognized that the loss of Verdun might well be enough to knock them out of the war – was a dreadful waste of an opportunity for some sort of triumph. Within days, the French had replenished their beleaguered defences, and the Somme offensive diverted the main thrust of German operations along the Western Front.

There was to be no other chance at Verdun for inflicting any kind of destabilizing blow against the French. By July, the Germans' inferiority in men and resources would keep them pegged to a defensive footing. The wider picture offered no further solace. The Germans were fighting alongside two allies – Turkey and Austria-Hungary – who were both showing signs of military weakness and, further, were struggling to deal with increasingly debilitating internal problems. On the other hand, France had behind it the British – recently bolstered in manpower by the introduction of conscription – and their imperial resources, as well as the Russians who, despite mounting domestic problems of their own, could for the time being call upon an army of vast proportions. Furthermore, each of France's allies had done its best to relieve the pressure at Verdun: the Italians at Isonzo; the Russians with Brusilov's offensive; and the British on the Somme. In contrast, Germany's allies had tended merely to hinder its operations on the Meuse.

The Germans ultimately failed to win through at Verdun because they did not concentrate their efforts in the necessary manner nor at the critical times. Moreover, Falkenhayn failed to realize the extent of France's ability – as a result of the *Noria* system – to sustain heavy losses at Verdun. Certainly, he fell into the trap of overestimating the formidability of his own infantry and artillery while underestimating those of the enemy. As a result of the failure, his actions at every level became subject to serious questioning: his omitting to inform Bethmann-Hollweg and, more crucially, Conrad and other German commanding Generals engaged elsewhere in the war, of the assault before it was begun; the facts that his strategic conceptions were ambiguous and that he sent the commander of the operation, the Crown Prince, into battle with a markedly different goal from his own; and, ultimately, his inability to capture the fortress and/or call off the offensive when the total costs attached to it reached prohibitive proportions.

Still, the German government was reluctant to admit that the onslaught against Verdun had been a massive calamity. As late as October, the Prussian Minister for War, von Hohenborn, was informing the Reichstag that the French had, indeed, been 'bled to death' in front of Verdun. He failed to mention, however, that the same was true of the German forces there. The army hierarchy, meanwhile, attempted a fudge of ludicrous proportions, suggesting that, in an era of modern industrial warfare, traditional conceptions, such as defeat and victory, no longer had meaning. But no one was very convinced by such statements, and the rhetoric did little to change the reality that the Germans had sustained horrific losses in their failed quest for Verdun.

The French ended 1916 the same as they had started the year, in possession of Verdun. But to do so had cost them dearly. Never before had a holding operation seen so many hundreds of thousands slaughtered, nor such a huge rearguard effort been mounted on French soil. Amid the rejoicing, questions began to be asked. Mainly, people sought an answer to why the theoretically most heavily defended fortified zone in France – if not in the world – had been left so weakened and vulnerable to attack.

They did not have to look far to find an answer. Foremost, too much had been left to chance. Inexcusably for a region that was a prominent part of the Western Front, the Verdun sector had been left under-resourced in men and in artillery. Furthermore, when intelligence sources began to suggest that the region might become the focus for an enemy attack, the reports were not acted upon until it was almost too late. The blame for this lies wholly with Joffre. He refused to believe that Verdun could become the object of a German offensive, apparently for no better reason than that it did not fit into his strategic conceptions of how the campaign was unfolding along the Western Front. This was a major oversight which was to cost the French immeasurable losses that they could ill afford and barely hope to sustain.

The obstinate refusal of the French General Staff to recognize that their doctrines were not working at Verdun resulted in more unnecessary casualties. Time after time, common sense dictated that the Germans be allowed to keep temporary possession of lost ground until men became available to mount a serious counter-move. But the command at Verdun continued to demand immediate, yet fatally under-resourced, attacks to try to recover lost ground quickly. Tens of thousands were sacrificed in this way. Furthermore, the dogmas of the few meant that tactical withdrawals, which would have offered strategic advantages, were never undertaken. The net result was the continued engagement of troops in ever more demoralizing skirmishes that could reap few tangible rewards.

The earlier down-grading of the Verdun fortifications was a mistake from which the French did not recover until the autumn of 1916, and then only at enormous expense. The decision was made in the context of the war as it had unfolded before 1915. It was a choice influenced by concerns about men and materials, and based on the seemingly irrefutable evidence of the ease with which the Belgian forts had been overrun in 1914. But events at Verdun were to show that the decision had been hastily made and that, further, it lacked foresight. The calamitous fall of Fort Douaumont, and the successes enjoyed by the Germans during their occupancy of it, would bear this out. As Pétain never tired of pointing out, the position should 'never have fallen into enemy hands', and, moreover, he felt that, if it had been properly defended to begin with, it 'would have discouraged the enemy from the start'.

Nevertheless, despite the poor defensive capacities of Verdun, once de Castlenau had made the decision in late February to maintain all positions before Verdun, there was really only one route open to the French General Staff: to defend the city and its forward-lying areas to the end regardless of material costs. Consequently, the battle quickly took on a symbolic significance far beyond its actual importance, and the fate of the French Army, the government, even the nation itself, became tied up in its outcome. By June it was evident that the loss of Verdun would spell disaster for France, and it is unlikely whether the country would have been able to pursue the war to a victorious end if the region had fallen during 1916.

Of course, events would have been much different if de Castlenau had not reached the hasty decision that he did. The abandonment of Verdun would almost certainly have been beneficial to the general French war effort. The terrain behind the city was perfectly defensible, and the Germans could not have advanced across it without committing themselves fully to such an operation. Furthermore, valuable reserves of infantry and artillery could have been saved for use at another point of engagement. The complexion of the war would have been radically altered and, arguably, the eventual defeat of Germany in the west brought about at a much earlier date. But other counsels prevailed.

The Battle of Verdun was very much controlled by the actions of the artillery. The French gained a sustainable upper hand only once they had established the supremacy of their heavy guns. It must be recognized, however, that, without the prolonged sacrifice by the infantry, the French would never have been able to give their heavy guns the chance to undermine the enemy's forces. Had the *poilus* not contested every centimetre of ground, the French General Staff would never have been able to organize the defence of Verdun.

On the face of it, then, the French were the clear victors at Verdun. Most neutrals had been appalled by reports of the savagery of the German assault on Verdun in February, and were happy to applaud an apparent instance of good triumphing over evil. French politicians and the army hierarchy pronounced a resounding victory and, perhaps rightly, revelled in the fact that they had been able to thwart the best efforts of the enemy. But there was a hollow ring to the eulogies. The costs had been so high, the consequences so horrific, that there was in truth little to celebrate. The triumph was an empty one, marred by the unknown dead still scattered across the fields of Lorraine. (The remains of the dead would later be collected and laid to rest at the haunting ossuary at Douaumont.) The writer, Jacques Meyer, considered Verdun a French victory 'only in the sense of an invincible resistance'. It is a conclusion not easily denied.

Furthermore, the battle may have been won but the war was little affected, at least not in the immediate term. The miracle breakthrough, which protagonists on all sides had sought at the turn of the year, had still not materialized by the end of it. The strategic deadlock along the Western Front was still in place and would remain so for a considerable time. Many contemporary observers were able to recognize that Verdun was but one horrific chapter in a book that was still being written.

There was a macabre futility to the human sacrifices wrought by the Battle of Verdun. The German Chancellor posed the question: 'where does incompetence end and criminality begin?' The answer was a murky one to which no individual had an adequate reply. At Verdun, all semblance of reason had taken flight. In the context of World War I, one commentator felt, 'The holocaust of Verdun was never exceeded and seldom equalled'. The poet, Paul Valéry, thought the battle was 'a complete war' within the wider conflict, and spoke of it as amounting to 'a single and almost symbolic fight'. There was a callousness, a lack of human understanding, attached to the entire affair that gave a bitter edge to the conflict. Falkenhayn admitted to looking at the monthly mortality figures much as a businessman looks at his balance sheets. That, he said, was 'just what this war is'.

The battle was a tragedy for all concerned. In its aftermath, the French talked of it as a 'glorious' victory. By the same token, the Germans could view it as nothing other than a national tragedy. This is how generations to come in both countries would speak, think, and write of it.

In France, the tangible consequence of Verdun and other episodes along the Western Front was the building in the inter-war years of the Maginot Line, a barrier of defensive fortifications to protect against the 'traditional' Teuton enemy. Less tangibly, Verdun entered the national psyche as an episode of great national valour, an event to be considered in the same bracket as Roncevaux and Valmy. Verdun became enshrouded in a mythical notion of Eternal Glory, and this was often evoked by patriots and nationalists.

But there is no doubt that the process by which Verdun became woven into the French national psyche was encouraged by some, especially the military hierarchy, for it inevitably served to disguise the terrible memories of other, less glorious wartime episodes: the failure of Plan XVII, Artois, Champagne, Chemin des Dames. These reverses and failures were forgotten in the glimmering shadow of the valiant defence of Verdun. In his memoirs of the battle, Pétain spoke of Verdun as representing 'the moral bulwark of France'. Such overly sentimental accolades only slowly detached themselves in France from popular recollections of the battle.

But Verdun also haunted the memories of thousands, and bred a kind of cynicism and loss of vitality – especially in the armed forces – that shaped the world view of an entire generation. Philip Guedalla observed that, in holding Verdun, the French 'lost something far more irreplaceable', and that 'to this extent the German move succeeded'. This was to have far-reaching consequences when the Germans again came 'knocking' at France's eastern gate in 1940.

The Germans were more reserved in their testaments to Verdun. Hindenburg thought the battle represented 'a beacon light of German valour'. But not many others made such elevated statements. For those who had survived the campaign, Verdun remained a ghastly spectre from which it was hard to escape. The place became christened 'the slaughterhouse of Germany', and that was how it was popularly remembered. For some of those who had not been there but had lived through the bitter experience of the defeat, it remained a shameful example of the brutality with which Imperial Germany pursued its war aims. For the German military, however – which remained remarkably unchanged at the top level after the war – there were important tactical and strategic lessons to be learned from the defeat. Again, these were of no small significance in 1940.

Verdun remains symbolic of the routine, unforgiving slaughter that typified World War I. The battle was just one event in an affair that everywhere exacted a similar grim harvest of casualties. But perhaps

The ossuary at Douaumont, final resting place for the unidentified dead of the Verdun battlefield

Verdun was the grimmest episode of all, a tragedy that wrought unnecessary horrors and inflicted unprecedented fatalities. The writer, Maurice Genevoix, who served at Verdun and went on to become a vehement campaigner for peace, stated: 'What we did is more than men could be asked, yet we did it'. Whether any army, from any generation or country, could do it again is open to question. From the perspective of more than eighty years, it seems unlikely.

Today, Verdun continues to resonate with a heavy symbolism. In 1984, the leaders of Germany and France chose it as the spot to announce reconciliation and ever-closer political, economic, and social ties between the two nations. In 1987, the United Nations bestowed upon the city the title, 'World Capital of Peace, Freedom and Human Rights'. It stands as a beacon of peace and reconciliation, and its 'eternal fame', created by the events there in 1916 and first spoken of by Jacques Meyer in the immediate aftermath of the battle, is as strong today as ever. Yet the memories of that year continue to reverberate. The ghosts of the past still haunt the soil of this corner of Europe.

Further Reading

Although matters are slowly changing, there has been a dearth of specialist material on Verdun available in the English language in recent years. This is possibly because the battle did not directly concern the British, and almost certainly because Alistair Horne's *The Price of Glory: Verdun 1916*, has achieved the status of being a seminal text. Since its publication in 1962, the book has never been out of print. Translated histories of the Battle of Verdun, comparable in scope to Horne's, are now mostly unavailable. Nevertheless, Georges Blond's *Verdun* (1967) is worth seeking out.

General texts on World War I, which provide valuable background information as well as analyses of the Battle of Verdun, are widely available in English. The best of these are Martin Gilbert's *First World War* (1994) and, more recently, John Keegan's *The First World War* (1998). H. H. Herwig's *The First World War: Germany and Austria* (1997) offers a unique, and often neglected, view of the war – and, indeed, Verdun – from the German point of view. Similarly, Lyn Macdonald's *The Roses of No Man's Land* (1980) offers a valuable insight into the provision of aid for the wounded French at Verdun. Some older texts remain useful for the incisiveness of their analysis: A. J. P. Taylor's *The First World War: An Illustrated History* (1963); Winston Churchill's *The World Crisis* (five volumes and various editions, though an abridged paperback is available); and B. H. Liddell Hart's *History of the World War, 1914–18* (1934).

Memoirs are a valuable, though not always reliable, source of information on the Battle of Verdun, and many of the main protagonists on both sides produced them. Again, these are no longer readily available but can be found in many public and institutional libraries. Pétain's *Verdun* (1930) is unique in its conciseness; Joffre's *Memoirs* (1932) and Falkenhayn's *General Headquarters, 1914–16, and its Critical Decisions* (1919) are both marked by their stunning detachment from the full horrors of the battle for Verdun. The Crown Prince's *Memoirs* and *My War Experiences* (both 1922) are slightly more emotive on the subject of Verdun.

Novelists in France and in Germany used Verdun to great effect after the war. Sadly, most works, such as Arnold Zweig's *Education Before Verdun*, are no longer in circulation although Jules Romain's *Verdun* has recently been republished by Prion in London. Though not directly concerned with Verdun, Erich Maria Remarque's *All Quiet On The Western Front* remains essential reading for anyone interested in the psychological impact of World War I on those men commanded to serve on that front.

Index

MILITARY HISTORY BOOKS

LETTERS HOME FROM THE CRIMEA
A young cavalryman's campaign
Edited by Philip Warner
Paperback £9.99

THE LETTERS OF PRIVATE WHEELER 1809–1828
An eyewitness account of the Battle of Waterloo
Edited and with a foreword by B. H. Liddell Hart
'*Vivid images – of people, landscape, events – flow from his pen . . .
one of military history's great originals*'
John Keegan
Paperback £9.99

THE DIARY OF A NAPOLEONIC FOOT SOLDIER
Jakob Walter
A conscript in the *Grande Armée*'s account of the long march home on the
retreat from Moscow
Edited and Introduced by Marc Raeff
Paperback £9.99 Illustrated

THE RECOLLECTIONS OF RIFLEMAN HARRIS
One of the most popular military books of all time
Edited and Introduced by Christopher Hibbert
'*An ordinary soldier's memoirs are rare but precious. Harris's are a most
vivid record of the war in Spain and Portugal against Napoleon, the same campaign
as featured in the recent TV drama series, 'Sharpe'.*'
The Mail on Sunday
Paperback £9.99

THE GREAT CIVIL WAR
A Military History of the First Civil War
Alfred H. Burne & Peter Young
Paperback £9.99

SOMEONE HAS BLUNDERED
Calamities of the British Army in the Victorian Age
Denis Judd
Paperback £6.99

THE WHEATLEY DIARY
A Journal & Sketchbook from the Peninsular War &
The Waterloo Campaign
Edited and Introduced by Christopher Hibbert
Paperback £10.99 Illustrated in colour